Texas Assessment Preparation

Grade 10

HOLT McDOUGAL

Literature

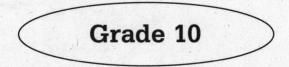

Texas

TEXAS

WRITE

SOURCE

 HOUGHTON MIFFLIN HARCOURT

W9-AFU-843

Copyright © by Houghton Mifflin Harcourt Publishing Company

All rights reserved. No part of this work may be reproduced or transmitted in any form or by any means, electronic or mechanical, including photocopying or recording, or by any information storage or retrieval system, without the prior written permission of the copyright owner unless such copying is expressly permitted by federal copyright law.

Permission is hereby granted to individuals using the corresponding student's textbook or kit as the major vehicle for regular classroom instruction to photocopy entire pages from this publication in classroom quantities for instructional use and not for resale. Requests for information on other matters regarding duplication of this work should be addressed to Houghton Mifflin Harcourt Publishing Company, Attn: Contracts, Copyrights, and Licensing, 9400 South Park Center Loop, Orlando, Florida 32819.

Printed in the U.S.A.

ISBN 978-0-547-74913-6

1 2 3 4 5 6 7 8 9 10   0982   20 19 18 17 16 15 14 13 12 11

4500305993   A B C D E F G

If you have received these materials as examination copies free of charge, Houghton Mifflin Harcourt Publishing Company retains title to the materials and they may not be resold. Resale of examination copies is strictly prohibited.

Possession of this publication in print format does not entitle users to convert this publication, or any portion of it, into electronic format.

Contents

© Houghton Mifflin Harcourt Publishing Company

Written Composition

Revising and Editing

PART II: *TEXAS WRITE SOURCE* ASSESSMENTS

Contents

© Houghton Mifflin Harcourt Publishing Company

How to Use This Book

Texas Assessment Preparation contains instruction that will help you develop the reading and writing skills tested on the State of Texas Assessments of Academic Readiness (STAAR). In addition, this book includes tests that accompany the Houghton Mifflin Harcourt *Texas Write Source* program.

PART I: PREPARING FOR TEXAS ASSESSMENTS

Part I of the book will help you develop skills assessed on the STAAR test. It consists of two basic types of instruction:

- **Guided instruction** materials offer annotations, citations from the Texas Essential Knowledge and Skills (TEKS), and answer explanations, plus models and rubrics for written composition. Annotations highlight the key skills you will need to apply. Sample questions, answer explanations, models, and rubrics help you analyze each question or prompt and its correct response.

- **Practice** materials give you the opportunity to apply what you have learned to assessments like those you will be taking near the end of your school year.

Part I is divided into the following sections:

Reading

The readings from a variety of genres give you opportunities to practice the essential reading skills outlined in the TEKS for your grade. Initially, as you read the Guided Reading passages, annotations and shading offer detailed explanations that draw attention to specific TEKS-based skills. After you have finished reading, you may review and hone test-taking skills by analyzing sample multiple-choice items, their answers, and answer explanations. You may also analyze short-answer questions with high-scoring response rubrics and sample answers. Following guided instruction, you will independently practice essential reading and assessment skills. For these Reading Practice lessons, you will read selections and answer multiple-choice items and short-answer questions that cover a range of appropriate TEKS and reading comprehension skills.

One feature of the Reading Practice materials in this book is a column headed "**My notes about what I am reading.**" You can improve your comprehension skills by using this column to monitor your reading abilities.

As you read the Reading Practice selections, take advantage of the "My notes about what I am reading" column by using it to make notes about the following topics.

- Key ideas or events

- Initial or overall impressions of characters, situations, or topics, including how each is like someone or something familiar to you

- Guesses at the meaning of any unfamiliar words or phrases

- Questions or points of confusion

- Ideas about why the author wrote the selection

- Comments about what you would like to know more about
- Your own ideas about the meaning of ideas or events or how they might apply to the real world

In addition, you may want to mark the selection text itself. You can, for example, circle, underscore, or highlight words or phrases that seem important or about which you have questions.

Written Composition

This section provides you with model essay prompts, sample essays, and scoring rubrics. These resources give you opportunities to practice the writing process for genres that will be tested. First, annotations will guide you as you analyze sample prompts and 2- and 4-point model responses. Then, you will practice your writing skills independently by responding to similar TEKS-aligned prompts.

Revising and Editing

In the multiple-choice format of this section, you will practice TEKS-based revising and editing skills. First, you will receive guided instruction in revising or editing. You will read sample essays, review assessment items, and analyze answer explanations. Then, you will work on independent practice, in which you identify editing or revising issues in sample essays and answer multiple-choice items crafted to cover a range of appropriate revising or editing TEKS.

PART II: *TEXAS WRITE SOURCE* ASSESSMENTS

The *Texas Write Source* assessments are a set of four tests designed to help you measure your progress in *Texas Write Source*.

- The **Pretest** should be completed at the beginning of the school year. It can help you measure your level of writing experience and knowledge and what your teacher might need to emphasize in your instruction. The **Pretest** also provides a baseline for measuring your progress from the beginning of the year to the end.

- **Progress Test 1** and **Progress Test 2** should be completed at regular intervals during the year. These tests can help you and your teacher monitor your progress as the school year proceeds.

- The **Post-test** should be completed at the end of the year to show how much progress you have made.

Each test has three parts. *Part 1: Improving Sentences and Paragraphs* and *Part 2: Correcting Sentence Errors* comprise a total of 32 multiple-choice questions. You will choose the best answer to each question. *Part 3: Writing* provides a writing prompt. You respond by writing a composition.

> NOTE: Every effort has been made to incorporate the latest information available about STAAR at the time of publication.

Part I

Preparing for Texas Assessments

Guided Reading

Reading Literary Text: Fiction

In this part of the book, you will read a short story with instruction about the elements of fiction. Following the selection are sample questions and answers about the story. The purpose of this section is to show you how to understand and analyze fiction.

To begin, review the TEKS that relate to fiction:

FICTION TEKS	WHAT IT MEANS TO YOU
(5) Comprehension of Literary Text/Fiction Students understand, make inferences and draw conclusions about the structure and elements of fiction and provide evidence from text to support their understanding. Students are expected to:	
(A) analyze isolated scenes and their contribution to the success of the plot as a whole in a variety of works of fiction;	You will examine specific scenes in fictional works and analyze how successfully those scenes advance the plot.
(B) analyze differences in the characters' moral dilemmas in works of fiction across different countries or cultures;	You will analyze the different ways characters respond to moral dilemmas in works of fiction from different countries and cultures.
(C) evaluate the connection between forms of narration (e.g., unreliable, omniscient) and tone in works of fiction; and	You will evaluate how the author's choice of a narrator affects the tone of works of fiction.
(D) demonstrate familiarity with works by authors from non-English-speaking literary traditions with emphasis on 20th century world literature.	You will become familiar with works by authors who come from peoples whose first language is not English, especially those from the 20th century.

The selection that follows provides instruction on the fiction TEKS as well as other TEKS. It also covers reading comprehension skills, such as summarizing and making inferences about text.

As you read the story "In the Sun Room," notice how the author uses several isolated scenes to develop the plot and characters. The annotations in the margins will guide you as you read.

© Houghton Mifflin Harcourt Publishing Company

Name _____ Date _____

Guided Reading

Read this selection. Then answer the questions that follow.

In the Sun Room

1   Ana sat at a table, tapping her feet to music, making a birthday card for her little brother. Next to her was a bowl of strawberries. Every time she popped one in her mouth, she thought of summer in the backyard.

2   Ana and her brother Jamie loved to spend hours kicking a soccer ball through the grass and spinning until they were dizzy on an old tire tied to a tree limb. Ana was bigger and stronger, and she could always kick the ball a little farther and run a little faster. But Jamie never stopped trying to keep up with her, laughing the entire time. In the afternoon, they would sit in the bright sunroom of their house eating their way through a bowl of ripe strawberries and flipping through comic books with sticky, red fingertips. Ana couldn't wait for it to be summer again! But today she was mostly excited about Jamie's birthday.

3   "Jamie is eight years old today," she thought to herself, "and Mom will make him a cake." He loved chocolate cake with a pinch of cinnamon and chocolate icing. Imagining his smile smeared in frosting, she got back to work on her card. In front of her was a large piece of blue construction paper, piles of stubby crayons, a bottle of white glue, and sheets of brightly colored tissue paper. She tried to shape the tissue paper into flowers. Then she plopped them into puddles of glue on the construction paper. While the flowers dried, she wrapped Jamie's gifts—a comic book and a red racecar that zipped across the floor by itself after you dragged it backwards. She knew Jamie liked to disappear into a comic book and pretend he was a superhero. And he always dreamed of driving a racecar so he could finally be faster than all the other kids his age.

4   Ana looked forward to the day when Jamie actually would be stronger and faster. Then the bigger boys wouldn't tease him on the school playground or at gym class. He could go to school every day and not have to stay home in bed when he was feeling too sick and weak to get dressed. Their days of playing outside together during the summer would not have to be interrupted by trips to the doctor or to the hospital.

POINT OF VIEW
From paragraph 1, you know that this story is told from the third-person point of view. The narrator refers to the character Ana with the pronouns *she* and *her* and also tells what Ana is thinking. As you read, decide whether the narrator reveals only Ana's thoughts and feelings or is omniscient—able to describe all the characters' thoughts and feelings.

TEKS 5C

MAKING INFERENCES
When you combine textual evidence with your own knowledge and experience, you can make an inference—or logical guess—about the characters in a story. For example, clues in paragraphs 3–4 allow you to infer that Ana's brother Jamie has a serious, long-term illness.

Fig. 19B

GO ON

5   To Ana, the doctor's office and the hospital were cold, gray places. Her mother had to take the highway through the city to get there, and the car was either stiflingly hot or too cold. There was always traffic. Mom would snap at them to stop arguing, talking, laughing, or singing in the back seat. She was a different person on those days. Worry lines creased her forehead, and she gripped the steering wheel as if she were trying to bend it into another shape. Jamie always seemed smaller and sicker to Ana after those trips, too. But she didn't have time to think about that. Today was his birthday and there was going to be a party.

6   Ana finished her card and stood up. The cake was ready, its scent of cinnamon and chocolate in the air. The strawberries were in bowls on the table. Maybe they could play pin-the-tail-on-the-donkey. She had already asked Mom to help her iron her favorite yellow dress. The dress brought back fond memories of the day she got it, on a family trip to the department store one weekend. She and Jamie walked by racks of clothing and pretended they were all grown up with lots of money, shopping for themselves. Then Ana, Jamie, Mom, and Dad went to a restaurant and had pizza and chocolate milk. They laughed about the man behind the counter, who had flour in his hair and told loud jokes to the customers. That day, Jamie was feeling great, which meant everybody was happy. Ana couldn't wait for more days like those! She sat back down in her chair and looked out the window while she waited for Jamie.

SYMBOLISM

A symbol is an object in a story that stands for itself but also for something else. To interpret a symbol, such as the strawberries in paragraph 6, think about what it means to the characters or why it is important to them.

TEKS 7

7   Jason Vargas parked his car, walked up the steps of Clover Hill Nursing Home, and pushed open the big glass doors. He carried flowers and two pints of fresh strawberries. One of his mother's nurses walked by holding a tray of medications.

8   "Hi there, Mr. Vargas. Your mother is in the sunroom, as usual," she said, smiling. "She's all ready for you!"

9   "Thank you, Mrs. Peters," Jason answered. "How is she today?"

ANALYZING SCENES

In a short story, writers often signal the start of a new scene with a text feature, such as the larger space between paragraphs 6 and 7. In the second scene of this story, the narrator introduces a new character, Jason Vargas. Continue reading to find out how he is connected to Ana and Jamie.

TEKS 5A

10   "Well, cheerful as always, birthday boy—she's been working hard all morning getting ready to party with you—dressing up, making cards, dusting the sunroom." Nurse Peters laughed. "I brought out her box of stuff from the closet so she could find something to wrap. And she made me get some cupcakes from the vending machine. They HAD to be chocolate. She even asked if I could find some cinnamon to sprinkle on them. 'That's Jamie's favorite,' she said. I said to her, 'Ana, that boy of yours is so lucky. You are one special mom.'"

11   Jason sighed. He gave a worried smile. "Well, she is special," he said. "But, actually, it's not my birthday today. Jamie is her brother."

12   "Really? I assumed that was her nickname for you," said Nurse Peters.

13   "Jamie was her brother. He was always sick. He died when he was eight and she was eleven. They were very close, and her whole family was never the same after they lost him. I think she spent a lot of years trying to forget him, and now for some reason the Alzheimer's has been taking her back to him." Jason paused. "Well, thanks, Mrs. Peters, I should go to her . . ."

14   Jason made his way down the hall to the sunroom where his mother was sitting. She was in a chair looking out the big windows, clutching her wrapped gifts and her bowl of strawberries. He wanted to cry for her. But then she turned around to look at him. He saw that her smile was full and loving. The sun room was as bright and warm as a summer's day. Returning his mother's smile, he walked in to celebrate Jamie's eighth birthday and enjoy chocolate and strawberries in the sun.

NARRATION AND TONE
What the narrator tells readers about characters in a story often reveals a particular tone, or attitude, toward the characters. In paragraph 14, the narrator tells readers what Jason is thinking and feeling as he enters his mother's room. These details help create the story's tone.

TEKS 5C

Use "In the Sun Room" (pp. 5–7) to answer questions 1–6.

1 Read this passage from the story.

> *To Ana, the doctor's office and the hospital were cold, gray places. Her mother had to take the highway through the city to get there, and the car was either stiflingly hot or too cold. There was always traffic. Mom would snap at them to stop arguing, talking, laughing, or singing in the back seat. She was a different person on those days. Worry lines creased her forehead, and she gripped the steering wheel as if she were trying to bend it into another shape.*

What inference can you make from the details in the passage?

A Jamie's illness caused stress and anxiety for his whole family.

B Ana and Jamie's mother was not accustomed to driving in the city.

C Ana and Jamie's father did not live with them.

D Jamie died from his illness.

EXPLANATION: The passage says that Ana considered the medical buildings to be "cold, gray places." Her mother "was a different person" on days when Jamie was very sick. From these clues and your own knowledge of how people react to worry and stress, you can infer that **A** is correct.
- **B** is incorrect. Though being unaccustomed to city driving could explain the mother's behavior, she probably made these trips frequently because Jamie was ill.
- **C** is incorrect. The fact that the father does not go along on hospital trips does not mean he does not live with the family. Work may keep him from making the trip.
- **D** is incorrect because the reader learns of Jamie's death later in the story. No details in the passage suggest that Jamie will die.

Fig. 19B

2 In the story, strawberries are a symbol of —

F Ana and Jamie's favorite food

G the strength to overcome a serious illness

H the love that connects Jamie, Ana, and Jason

J celebrating major family events, such as birthdays

EXPLANATION: A symbol represents something beyond itself. The strawberries relate to Ana's memories of spending time with her brother and to her desire to create a special birthday party for him. In the second scene of the story, Jason brings strawberries to the nursing home as a gesture of his love and concern for his mother. All of these connections show the family members' love for one another. **H** is correct.
- **F** is incorrect. The story suggests that strawberries are literally Ana and Jamie's favorite food, but this is not an example of symbolism.
- **G** is incorrect because the strawberries are related to Ana and Jamie's happy times together, not to Jamie's struggle with his illness.
- **J** is incorrect. Although the strawberries are related to birthday celebrations, they are also related to more ordinary days when Ana and Jamie read comic books together.

TEKS 7; Fig. 19B

GO ON

3 What does the scene between Jason and the nurse (paragraphs 7–13) contribute to the story as a whole?

A It explains why Jason brings strawberries to the nursing home and leads to the story's climax as he confronts his mother's memory loss.

B It reveals the pain that Jason feels over the loss of his uncle and helps explain his reluctance to visit his mother at the nursing home.

C It tells readers how the conflict involving Jamie's illness was resolved and shows readers what is really happening in Ana's present life.

D It creates a feeling of suspense because readers are unsure which version of reality—Ana's or Jason's—is correct.

> **EXPLANATION:** The conversation between Jason and the nurse reveals that the girl Ana is now old and living in a nursing home, and that her brother Jamie died when she was eleven. **C** is correct.
> - **A** is incorrect. Jason brings strawberries because his mother likes them; his conversation with the nurse provides no further details about this. The scene is not climactic; Jason's sigh in paragraph 11 suggests that he has already accepted his mother's condition.
> - **B** is incorrect. Jason never knew his uncle, and there is no evidence to indicate that he is reluctant to visit his mother.
> - **D** is incorrect. There is little doubt that Jason's version of reality is accurate and that Ana's is distorted. In the first scene, Ana is alone with her thoughts and memories, so there is no one else to confirm her perceptions. In the second scene, Jason and the nurse discuss what is really happening.

TEKS 5A

4 How does the form of narration in this story affect its tone, or express a particular attitude?

F The omniscient third-person narrator first describes Ana's perceptions and then Jason's, creating a tone of compassion for both characters.

G The limited third-person narrator shows how Jason suffers as a result of his mother's illness, creating a bitter tone about the unfairness of the situation.

H The omniscient third-person narrator reveals Ana's and Jason's feelings but not the nurse's, creating a critical tone toward the medical profession.

J The limited third-person narrator presents a rich picture of Ana's inner world and the happiness it brings her, creating a tone of doubt about the value of normal perceptions.

> **EXPLANATION:** A third-person narrator is outside the story. The narrator is limited if the thoughts and feelings of only one character are described, and omniscient if those of all the characters can be described. **F** is correct because the third-person narrator communicates the thoughts and feelings of both Ana and Jason. The overall effect is to show compassion for both of these characters who have suffered difficult losses.
> - **G** and **J** are incorrect because the narrator is not limited.
> - **H** is incorrect. Even though the nurse's thoughts and feelings are not described, there is nothing in the story to suggest a critical attitude toward her or the medical profession.

TEKS 5C; Fig. 19B

GO ON

5 In paragraph 14, Jason's mood changes from sad to contented because —

A he remembers that his mother has arranged for them to have chocolate cake with cinnamon

B he knows that Jamie is not really dead, and he looks forward to sharing this news with Ana

C he feels hopeful that Ana will overcome her Alzheimer's disease

D he realizes that his mother's memory loss has eased her suffering over Jamie's death

EXPLANATION: When Jason arrives at Ana's room, he has just finished a conversation with Nurse Peters about his mother's Alzheimer's and how it has made her confuse people and events from the past and present. This makes him feel sad and worried. However, Jason's mood changes when his mother turns to him with a "full and loving" smile. **D** is correct. Jason realizes that since his mother is not suffering over Jamie's death, they can be happy and enjoy the day together.
- **A** is incorrect. Chocolate cake with cinnamon was Jamie's favorite, not Jason's, and the thought of cake would not be enough to overcome Jason's sadness at his mother's illness.
- **B** is incorrect. Jamie died many years ago.
- **C** is incorrect. There is no evidence in the text to suggest that Jason feels hopeful about a cure for Alzheimer's disease.

Fig. 19B

6 Which of the following is the best summary of the story?

F A man visits his mother, who has Alzheimer's disease, in a nursing home. He is frustrated that she confuses him with her younger brother, who died many years ago. However, he resigns himself to celebrating the brother's birthday with her.

G A woman with Alzheimer's believes she is preparing a birthday celebration for her brother, who died many years ago. Instead, her son visits her. His first impulse is to feel sad, but then he sees that she is filled with love and happiness despite her memory loss.

H A girl prepares a birthday celebration for her little brother, to whom she is very close. As she wraps gifts and ensures that his favorite foods are laid out, she recalls some of her fondest memories of playing, reading, and shopping with her brother.

J A mother and son have two very different perceptions of the same event. She thinks it is a birthday party, while he thinks it is a reminder of a long-lost past. Finally, he decides to enjoy their time together, since she seems happy.

EXPLANATION: A summary tells the most important events in a story and accurately conveys how the conflict is resolved. **G** is correct because it summarizes both scenes of the story and tells how Jason feels at the story's conclusion.
- **F** is incorrect because the end of the story conveys Jason's love for his mother, not his frustration over her memory loss.
- **H** is incorrect. The summary is incomplete because it focuses on details from the first scene in the story but omits the second scene. It also leaves out the important fact that Ana is no longer a little girl, even though she thinks she is.
- **J** is incorrect. It does not give enough details—such as the fact that the mother suffers from memory loss and that the party is for a brother who is dead—for readers to understand the story's plot.

TEKS 5; Fig. 19A

GO ON

Answer the following question in the space provided.

7 What is the main conflict or problem in the story "In the Sun Room"? Is it successfully resolved? Explain your answer and support it with evidence from the story.

EXPLANATION
Rubric, high-scoring response:
- Reflects a perceptive awareness of text meaning and complexities; makes meaningful connections across the text
- Uses specific, well-chosen evidence from the text, supporting validity of response
- Shows deep understanding of the text through ideas and supporting text evidence

Sample Response: The main conflict in the story is Ana's struggle with Alzheimer's disease. She lives in the past with her childhood memories of her brother. She forgets that he has died and "[looks] forward to the day when Jamie actually would be stronger and faster," after he recovers from his illness. This confusion and memory loss isolate her from her son and other people who live in the present. The conflict reaches a climax when Jason comes her room and she turns around. Will she be disappointed and sad that he is not her brother Jamie, for whom she has prepared a birthday celebration? As it turns out, her memory loss protects her from feeling sad on Jamie's birthday. She smiles warmly at Jason, who enters the room to celebrate with her, creating a satisfying resolution to the story.

TEKS 5A, 5B; Fig. 19B

Reading Literary Text: Literary Nonfiction

In this part of the book, you will read a speech with instruction about the elements of literary nonfiction. Following the selection are sample questions and answers about the speech. The purpose of this section is to show you how to understand and analyze literary nonfiction.

To begin, review the TEKS that relate to literary nonfiction:

LITERARY NONFICTION TEKS	WHAT IT MEANS TO YOU
(6) Comprehension of Literary Text/Literary Nonfiction Students understand, make inferences and draw conclusions about the varied structural patterns and features of literary nonfiction and provide evidence from text to support their understanding. Students are expected to evaluate the role of syntax and diction and the effect of voice, tone, and imagery on a speech, literary essay, or other forms of literary nonfiction.	You will understand and draw conclusions about the structure and elements of literary nonfiction and back up your analysis using examples from the text. You will also evaluate how an author's sentence structure, word choice, voice, tone, and use of imagery affect the message of a speech, literary essay, or other nonfiction work.

The selection that follows provides instruction on the literary nonfiction TEKS as well as other TEKS. It also covers reading comprehension skills, such as making complex inferences and supporting them with textual evidence.

As you read the excerpt from the speech "The Indian's Night Promises to Be Dark," notice how the author's choice of words and images conveys a particular tone or attitude toward his topic. The annotations in the margins will guide you as you read.

© Houghton Mifflin Harcourt Publishing Company

Guided Reading

Read this selection. Then answer the questions that follow.

---

from The Indian's Night Promises to Be Dark

by Chief Seattle

Chief Seattle was a leader of the Suquamash people near Puget Sound in present-day Washington state. He befriended white settlers, working with them in the fishing business and negotiating treaties to promote cooperation. In 1854 or 1855, on the occasion of a treaty that would cede 2.5 million acres of land to the Americans, Chief Seattle is said to have given the following speech. The English translation was published in 1887, after Seattle's death.

1   Day and night cannot dwell together. The red man has ever fled the approach of the white man, as the changing mists on the mountain side flee before the blazing morning sun.

2   However, your proposition seems a just one, and I think my folks will accept it and will retire to the reservation you offer them, and we will dwell apart and in peace, for the words of the great white chief seem to be the voice of nature speaking to my people out of the thick darkness that is fast gathering around them like a dense fog floating inward from a midnight sea.

3   It matters but little where we pass the remainder of our days. They are not many. The Indian's night promises to be dark. No bright star hovers about the horizon. Sad-voiced winds moan in the distance. Some grim Nemesis of our race is on the red man's trail, and wherever he goes he will still hear the sure approaching footsteps of the fell destroyer and prepare to meet his doom, as does the wounded doe that hears the approaching footsteps of the hunter. A few more moons, a few more winters, and not one of all the mighty hosts that once filled this broad land or that now roam in fragmentary bands through these vast solitudes will remain to weep over the tombs of a people once as powerful and hopeful as your own.

IMAGERY
Imagery is language that appeals to the senses. In paragraph 1, Chief Seattle uses vivid imagery to compare his people's fate to that of a disappearing mist at sunrise.
TEKS 6

FIGURATIVE LANGUAGE
In paragraph 2, Seattle uses a figure of speech called a simile—a comparison with the word *like* or *as*. He compares the historical situation of his people to a familiar natural phenomenon on Puget Sound, the approach of a dense fog.
TEKS 2C

ALLUSION
An allusion is a reference to a well-known person, event, or literary work. In paragraph 4, Seattle makes an allusion to Nemesis, the ancient Greek goddess of vengeance. She pursued and punished people who had committed evil acts or who had enjoyed an unfair amount of happiness.
TEKS 7

GO ON ➡

4   But why should we repine[1]? Why should I murmur at the fate of my people? Tribes are made up of individuals and are no better than they. Men come and go like the waves of the sea. A tear, a tamanawus,[2] a dirge, and they are gone from our longing eyes forever. Even the white man, whose God walked and talked with him, as friend to friend, is not exempt from the common destiny. We *may* be brothers after all. We shall see.

5   We will ponder your proposition, and when we have decided we will tell you. But should we accept it, I here and now make this the first condition: That we will not be denied the privilege, without molestation, of visiting at will the graves of our ancestors and friends. Every part of this country is sacred to my people. Every hill-side, every valley, every plain and grove has been hallowed by some <u>fond</u> memory or some sad experience of my tribe.

6   Even the rocks that seem to lie dumb as they swelter in the sun along the silent seashore in solemn grandeur thrill with memories of past events connected with the fate of my people, and the very dust under your feet responds more lovingly to our footsteps than to yours, because it is the ashes of our ancestors, and our bare feet are conscious of the sympathetic touch, for the soil is rich with the life of our kindred.

7   The sable braves, and fond mothers, and glad-hearted maidens, and the little children who lived and rejoiced here, and whose very names are now forgotten, still love these solitudes, and their deep fastnesses at eventide grow shadowy with the presence of dusky spirits.[3] And when the last red man shall have perished from the earth and his memory among white men shall have become a myth, these shores shall swarm with the invisible dead of my tribe, and when your children's children shall think themselves alone in the field, the store, the shop, upon the highway or in the silence of the woods they will not be alone. In all the earth there is no place dedicated to solitude. At night, when the streets of your cities and villages shall be silent, and you think them deserted, they will throng with the returning hosts that once filled and still love this beautiful land. The white man will never be alone. Let him be just and deal kindly with my people, for the dead are not altogether powerless.

1. **repine:** to be discontent or to complain; to yearn for something.
2. **tamanawus:** a ceremony in which a guardian spirit is summoned, often when death is near.
3. **their deep fastnesses . . . dusky spirits:** in the evening, secret places are visited by the souls of the dead.

DICTION

Diction refers to a speaker's choice of words. A speaker's diction reflects a particular attitude toward his or her subject—also called tone. Seattle uses formal diction, giving his speech a serious tone. Think about how the tone would change if the first sentence of paragraph 5 read, "We'll think about what you said and get back to you."

TEKS 6

CONTEXT CLUES

A word's connotation is the emotion attached to it, as opposed to its denotation, or literal definition. For example, the word *throng* in paragraph 7 literally means "to fill with a crowd." However, because Seattle describes the deep love that his people have for the land, the word connotes a joyous gathering.

TEKS 1B

GO ON ➡

Use the excerpt from "The Indian's Night Promises to Be Dark" (pp. 13–14) to answer questions 1–6.

1 Read this excerpt from the speech.

> . . . I here and now make this the first condition: That we will not be denied the privilege, without molestation, of visiting at will the graves of our ancestors and friends.

What effect does this statement have on the speech?

A Its vivid imagery describes the Puget Sound region to listeners unfamiliar with the area.

B Its formal diction creates a serious tone to match a serious occasion.

C Its figurative language compares visiting ancestors' graves to a privilege.

D Its simple syntax demonstrates how unsophisticated Chief Seattle is.

EXPLANATION: The sentence clearly states a condition under which Chief Seattle's people will agree to give up their land. It is a solemn statement about something deeply important to the Suquamash, and its formal vocabulary and sentence structure reflect the serious topic. **B** is correct.
- **A** is incorrect. Imagery is the use of words and phrases that appeal to the senses. This sentence contains no sensory images.
- **C** is incorrect. Figurative language uses words in a nonliteral or imaginative way. This statement is straightforward and literal.
- **D** is incorrect. The syntax or arrangement of words in the sentence, as in the balance of the speech, reveals a sophisticated thinker.

TEKS 6

2 What is the purpose of Chief Seattle's allusion to Nemesis in paragraph 3?

F To entertain listeners with an interesting story from Greek mythology

G To show the similarities between the Christian religion and that of the ancient Greeks

H To argue against the cruelty of hunting, which he now understands because his people are in a position similar to that of a hunted deer

J To suggest that his people are facing an inescapable fate, like someone in a Greek myth who is hunted down and punished by Nemesis

EXPLANATION: Allusions help writers convey meaning by comparing the topic of their writing to something else with which their audience is familiar. Seattle expects his audience to know that Nemesis hunted down people whom the Greek gods wanted to punish. No one could escape Nemesis's justice. **J** is correct because Seattle's people also cannot escape their fate.
- **F** is incorrect. Seattle makes a brief reference to Nemesis but does not tell a story about her. He expects his audience to know enough of her story to understand his allusion.
- **G** is incorrect. Seattle makes no reference to the Christian religion.
- **H** is incorrect because Seattle does not argue that hunting is cruel. He mentions the wounded deer merely as another example of a creature that cannot escape its fate.

TEKS 7

GO ON

3 Which word best describes Chief Seattle's tone or attitude toward the white man's proposition?

A Defiant

B Resigned

C Fearful

D Neutral

EXPLANATION: To answer this question, you must make an inference based on evidence from the text as well as your own knowledge and experience. **B** is correct because Seattle makes several statements showing that he sees living on a reservation as inevitable for his people. For example, he says in paragraph 2 that "we will dwell apart and in peace."
- **A** is incorrect. Seattle is accepting rather than defiant.
- **C** is incorrect. Seattle's statements do not stress that he is fearful about the future.
- **D** is incorrect. Seattle says in paragraph 2 that the proposition is "a just one," so he is not neutral.

TEKS 6; Fig. 19B

4 Which statement from the speech most clearly reflects Chief Seattle's cultural background?

F *However, your proposition seems a just one, and I think my folks will accept it and will retire to the reservation you offer them, and we will dwell apart and in peace. . . .*

G *Even the white man, whose God walked and talked with him, as friend to friend, is not exempt from the common destiny.*

H *. . . the very dust under your feet responds more lovingly to our footsteps than to yours, because it is the ashes of our ancestors, and our bare feet are conscious of the sympathetic touch, for the soil is rich with the life of our kindred.*

J *Men come and go like the waves of the sea.*

EXPLANATION: Seattle's cultural background includes the beliefs and the way of life of his people. **H** is correct because it reflects the connection his people feel to the land and to their ancestors. They regard the soil of their homeland as far more than dirt; it is "rich with the life of our kindred."
- **F** is incorrect. It mentions a reservation, but reservations were created by white people and have nothing to do with the Suquamash culture.
- **G** is incorrect. It refers to the religion of "the white man" from an outsider's perspective, but this is not specifically the perspective of Native Americans.
- **J** is incorrect. This simile comparing the human life cycle to ocean waves is a universal observation that could be made by a person from any cultural background.

TEKS 2C

5 Which of the following sentences uses the word <u>fond</u> with the same connotation that it has in paragraph 5?

A I like most vegetables, but I'm especially fond of eggplant.

B The little girl picked up her kitten and smothered it with fond kisses.

C The young man was sustained by his fond hope of eventually being reunited with his family.

D Few peasants believed the fond notion that they would be rewarded for their back-breaking work.

> **EXPLANATION:** From the context of paragraph 5, you can tell that *fond* means "cherished" or "dearly valued." Clues in the text include words such as "sacred" and "hallowed." **C** is correct because a desire to be reunited with one's family would be cherished in the same way as a memory of one's heritage.
> - **A** is incorrect because liking a particular food is not a deep and treasured experience like the one Seattle describes.
> - **B** is incorrect. In this sentence, *fond* means "affectionate" and refers to the feeling a child has for a pet.
> - **D** is incorrect because the sentence uses *fond* to mean "foolish or misguided." This is the opposite of the way Seattle uses the word.

TEKS 1B

6 Read these sentences from the end of the speech.

> *At night, when the streets of your cities and villages shall be silent, and you think them deserted, they will throng with the returning hosts that once filled and still love this beautiful land. The white man will never be alone. Let him be just and deal kindly with my people, for the dead are not altogether powerless.*

What was Chief Seattle's likely purpose in ending the speech the way he did?

F To warn white listeners to respect the vanquished Native Americans

G To cause white listeners to be inspired by the example that Native Americans set

H To cause white listeners to become closer to nature

J To cause white listeners to change their decision to send Native Americans to reservations

> **EXPLANATION:** Purpose is conveyed by the words and images a speaker chooses. Phrases such as "returning hosts," "The white man will never be alone," and "the dead are not altogether powerless" warn listeners to respect the memory of a once-great culture. **F** is correct.
> - **G** is incorrect. Seattle is describing the absence of his people from the land rather than their actions.
> - **H** is incorrect. In this part of the speech, Seattle mentions but does not emphasize his people's closeness to nature.
> - **J** is incorrect. Seattle does not make any direct statements or use language that implies he wants white people to change their decision. In fact, he feels the decision is inevitable.

Fig. 19B

GO ON

Name _____ Date _____

7 What words would you use to describe the tone of Seattle's speech? Explain your answer and support it with evidence from the speech.

EXPLANATION
Rubric, high-scoring response:
- Reflects a perceptive awareness of text meaning and complexities; makes meaningful connections across the text
- Uses specific, well-chosen evidence from the text, supporting validity of response
- Shows deep understanding of the text through ideas and supporting text evidence

Sample Response: The tone of Seattle's speech is resigned and pessimistic but dignified, as shown by the language that he uses. His resignation to the fate of having his people move to a reservation is evident in statements such as "Day and night cannot dwell together" and "Some grim Nemesis of our race is on the red man's trail," which create strong visual images. His pessimism is shown by other vivid language, such as "The Indian's night promises to be dark." But there is also dignity in the speech. Seattle affirms the nobility and worth of his people by demanding that they be allowed to visit the graves of their ancestors in every part of the country, because the soil is "rich with the life of our kindred" and "responds more lovingly to our footsteps" than to the white man's.

TEKS 6; Fig. 19A, 19B

Reading Literary Text: Poetry

In this part of the book, you will read a poem with instruction about the elements of poetry. Following the selection are sample questions and answers about the poem. The purpose of this section is to show you how to understand and analyze poetry.

To begin, review the TEKS that relate to poetry:

POETRY TEKS	WHAT IT MEANS TO YOU
(3) Comprehension of Literary Text/Poetry Students understand, make inferences and draw conclusions about the structure and elements of poetry and provide evidence from text to support their understanding. Students are expected to analyze the structure or prosody (e.g., meter, rhyme scheme) and graphic elements (e.g., line length, punctuation, word position) in poetry.	You will understand and draw conclusions about the structure and elements of poetry and back up your analysis using examples from the text. You will also analyze how the structure and graphic elements of poetry affect how the poetry sounds and appears.

The selection that follows provides instruction on the poetry TEKS as well as other TEKS. It also covers reading comprehension skills, such as making complex inferences based on evidence in the text.

As you read the poem "An Obstacle," notice how the poet uses the elements of poetry. The annotations in the margins will guide you as you read.

© Houghton Mifflin Harcourt Publishing Company

Name _____ Date _____

Guided Reading

Read this selection. Then answer the questions that follow.

An Obstacle

by Charlotte Perkins Gilman

I was climbing up a mountain-path
    With many things to do,
Important business of my own,
    And other people's too,
5 When I ran against a Prejudice
    That quite cut off the view.

My work was such as could not wait,
    My path quite clearly showed,
My strength and time were limited,
10   I carried quite a load,
And there that hulking Prejudice
    Sat all across the road.

So I spoke to him politely,
    For he was huge and high,
15 And begged that he would move a bit
    And let me travel by—
He smiled, but as for moving!—
    He didn't even try.

And then I reasoned quietly
20   With that colossal mule;
My time was short—no other path—
    The mountain winds were cool—
I argued like a Solomon,
    He sat there like a fool.

ELEMENTS OF POETRY
To determine a poem's meter, or pattern of stressed and unstressed syllables, read it aloud. After a few lines, you should notice a pattern that repeats throughout the poem. Also look for rhyming words, like *do, too,* and *view* in the first stanza, that create the rhyme scheme, or pattern of end rhymes.

TEKS 3

MAKING INFERENCES
Note that the speaker comes across "a Prejudice" in line 5. You can infer that the poem might be about more than literally climbing a mountain path.

Fig. 19B

ALLUSION
An allusion is a reference to a famous person, place, literary work, or event. In line 23, the poet refers to the Biblical king Solomon, who was known for his great wisdom.

TEKS 7

 GO ON

25   Then I flew into a passion,
       I danced and howled and swore,
    I pelted and belabored[1] him
       Till I was stiff and sore;
    He got as mad as I did—
30   But he sat there as before.

    And then I begged him on my knees—
       I might be kneeling still
    If so I hoped to move that mass
       Of obdurate ill-will—
35   As well invite the monument
       To vacate Bunker Hill![2]

    So I sat before him helpless,
       In an ecstasy of woe—
    The mountain mists were rising fast,
40   The sun was sinking slow—
    When a sudden inspiration came,
       As sudden winds do blow.

    I took my hat, I took my stick,
       My load I settled fair,
45   I approached that awful incubus[3]
       With an absent-minded air—
    And I walked directly through him,
       As if he wasn't there!

> **THEME**
> This poem has a narrative structure with a conflict and a resolution. The way the speaker's conflict is resolved in the last stanza reveals the poet's theme—the message about life that she wants to convey.
>
> **TEKS 2, 3, 5**

---

1. **pelted and belabored:** attacked with physical blows.
2. **Bunker Hill:** a reference to the first major battle of the Revolutionary War, fought in 1775 on Breed's Hill (near Bunker Hill) overlooking Boston Harbor. A 221-foot stone monument was erected on the site in 1825.
3. **incubus:** a heavy burden.

Name _____ Date _____

Use "An Obstacle" (pp. 20–21) to answer questions 1–6.

1 What obstacle does the speaker encounter?

A Prejudice

B Mountain winds

C A dangerous path

D Solomon

EXPLANATION: An obstacle is something that stands in the way. **A** is correct. The speaker is climbing up a mountain until "a Prejudice" blocks the path (lines 5–6).
• **B** is incorrect. The speaker describes the winds as cool (line 22) but does not say they are an obstacle.
• **C** is incorrect. The path is not described as dangerous.
• **D** is incorrect. The speaker compares herself to Solomon; Solomon is not an obstacle.

Fig. 19A

2 You could describe the rhyme scheme of this poem by stating that —

F every line in each stanza rhymes

G the first, third, and fifth lines of each stanza rhyme

H the second, fourth, and sixth lines of each stanza rhyme

J the poem has no clear rhyme scheme

EXPLANATION: The last word in the second, fourth, and sixth lines in each stanza rhyme. For example, in the first stanza, *do, too,* and *view* rhyme. **H** is correct.
• **F** is incorrect. Not every line rhymes. You can tell by looking at the last words in the first two lines: *path* and *do* do not rhyme.
• **G** is incorrect. The first, third, and fifth lines in each stanza never rhyme.
• **J** is incorrect. There is a pattern to the rhyme in this poem: the second, fourth, and sixth lines in each stanza rhyme.

TEKS 3

3 What is the effect of setting this poem on an uphill mountain path?

A It supports the speaker's opinion that the world is unsafe.

B It provides a beautiful background.

C It symbolizes the journey through life.

D It shows how physically fit the speaker is.

EXPLANATION: The speaker's challenge is to overcome "a Prejudice" while carrying out the important business of life. **C** is correct. This difficult task is symbolized by the speaker's climbing a mountain and encountering an obstacle in the path.
• **A** is incorrect. The speaker does not say the world is unsafe.
• **B** is incorrect. The speaker does not describe the scene as beautiful, and the poem's theme is not supported by placing the action in a beautiful setting.
• **D** is incorrect. The fitness of the speaker is not relevant to the poem's message.

TEKS 7; Fig. 19B

4 The poet uses the allusion to Solomon in line 23 to emphasize her message that —

F courtesy is the best way to win hearts

G intolerance doesn't respond to reason

H climbing a mountain is physically hard

J some people are very rude

EXPLANATION: Solomon represents wisdom and reason. The speaker tries, as Solomon would, to reason with Prejudice to make it move or change, to no avail. **G** is correct.
• **F** is incorrect. Solomon wasn't known for manners, nor do manners move "Prejudice."
• **H** is incorrect. Solomon has nothing to do with the speaker's symbolic climb.
• **J** is incorrect because it does not relate to Solomon's wisdom.

TEKS 7; Fig. 19B

GO ON

5 The word <u>obdurate</u> (line 34) comes from a Latin root meaning "hard." Using this information and the context in which the word is used in the poem, you can infer that *obdurate* means —

A built from stone

B unwilling to be persuaded

C extremely old

D cruel

> **EXPLANATION:** No matter how much the speaker begs, Prejudice will not move. Prejudice is "hard" in the sense of being impossible to persuade. **B** is correct.
> - **A** is incorrect. Unlike the Bunker Hill monument, Prejudice is not literally made of stone.
> - **C** is incorrect. The context does not suggest anything about Prejudice's age.
> - **D** is incorrect. Although Prejudice's behavior is causing the speaker pain, there is no evidence that he means to be cruel. He is merely stubborn.

TEKS 1A; Fig. 19B

6 What theme does the resolution of the speaker's conflict suggest?

F Most problems are imaginary, and they will disappear if people simply ignore them.

G Prejudice seems like a big problem in society, but it actually has no power to hurt people.

H Prejudices have power only if we choose to take them seriously.

J The best way to deal with a stubborn person is to pretend he or she does not exist.

> **EXPLANATION:** At the end of the poem, the speaker realizes that instead of fighting with Prejudice, the best way to get past him is to walk right through him. **G** is correct because Prejudice loses his power as soon as he is not taken seriously.
> - **F** is incorrect. The poem is about prejudice. Its message does not apply to all human problems.
> - **H** is incorrect. The speaker is hurt by the struggle with Prejudice, and the poet does not suggest that prejudices have no harmful effect on society.
> - **J** is incorrect. Although Prejudice is portrayed as a stubborn individual, the poet's message is about prejudice as an abstract quality.

TEKS 2, 3, 5; Fig. 19B

GO ON ➡

Answer the following question in the space provided.

7 Explain the personification in this poem. What idea is personified, or given human qualities? How does the poet use imagery to help you understand the idea?

EXPLANATION

Rubric, high-scoring response:

- Reflects a perceptive awareness of text meaning and complexities; makes meaningful connections across the text
- Uses specific, well-chosen evidence from the text, supporting validity of response
- Shows deep understanding of the text through ideas and supporting text evidence

Sample Response: Prejudice is personified in the poem. The poet describes how it "cut off the view" (line 6) and would not let the busy speaker by. She uses words such as *hulking, huge,* and *high* to describe Prejudice; he is a "colossal mule" (line 20) who will not move, despite the speaker's efforts. He smiles and sits "like a fool" (line 24) until the speaker attacks him physically, which makes him mad but still does not inspire him to move (lines 26–30). When the speaker begs, Prejudice shows only "obdurate ill-will" (line 34). These images help the reader understand that prejudice is a difficult, stubborn force that will not respond to reason, politeness, angry attacks, or desperate pleas.

TEKS 3, 7; Fig. 19B

Reading Literary Text: Drama

In this part of the book, you will read a play with instruction about the elements of drama. Following the selection are sample questions and answers about the play. The purpose of this section is to show you how to understand and analyze drama.

To begin, review the TEKS that relate to drama:

DRAMA TEKS	WHAT IT MEANS TO YOU
(4) Comprehension of Literary Text/Drama Students understand, make inferences and draw conclusions about the structure and elements of drama and provide evidence from text to support their understanding. Students are expected to analyze how archetypes and motifs in drama affect the plot of plays.	You will understand and draw conclusions about the structure and elements of drama and support your analysis with evidence from the text. You will also analyze how recurring patterns and character types (archetypes) and recurring themes (motifs) affect a play's story.

The selection that follows provides instruction on the drama TEKS as well as other TEKS. It also covers reading comprehension skills, such as making complex inferences about text.

As you read the play *Atlas and Hercules,* notice how the author uses dialogue and stage directions to tell a classic story from Greek mythology. The annotations in the margins will guide you as you read.

© Houghton Mifflin Harcourt Publishing Company

Guided Reading

Read this selection. Then answer the questions that follow.

Atlas and Hercules

CHARACTERS

Narrator

Hercules, an ancient Greek hero known for his great strength

Old Man of the Sea, a mysterious creature

Atlas, a giant who holds up the sky on his shoulders

(The stage is dark except for a spotlight stage right. Into this spotlight steps the NARRATOR.)

Narrator. Did you ever set your heart on a goal so challenging that you sometimes wondered if the struggle was
5 really worth it? Well, in the course of his twelve labors, the Greek hero Hercules must have had many such moments. Perhaps none was more full of uncertainty than when he set out to obtain the three golden apples from the garden of the Hesperides.

10 *(As the stage lights come up, we see HERCULES standing alone in a clearing. He is tall and muscle-bound with a proud bearing, although at this moment he appears tired.)*

Hercules. My future is a mystery, and my feet grow weary, but my spirit does not. When I angered the goddess Hera,
15 she caused me to lose my mind and kill my family. Now I must fulfill this quest or die trying. It is the only way I can relieve my awful guilt. So, I will carry on, searching for the Old Man of the Sea, who may hold the key to my success.

Narrator. Hercules trudged forward, uprooting massive trees
20 with single blows of his club to clear the path. Finally, reaching the beach, he saw a strange old man with scales and a long moldy beard, peacefully asleep on the sand.

ELEMENTS OF DRAMA
The cast of characters for this play includes a narrator. The narrator is not a character in the story but rather someone who gives the audience information about characters and events. In lines 5–9, the narrator introduces Hercules and his twelve labors. Stage directions, which appear in italic type, help readers imagine an actual performance of the play.

TEKS 4

ALLUSION
An allusion is a reference to a well-known person, place, event, or literary work. In line 14, Hercules makes an allusion to Hera. The playwright expects the audience to know Hera's story from Greek mythology. Hera was the wife of the god Zeus, and Hercules was Zeus's son with another woman. Because Hera was jealous of Zeus's other lovers, she made life difficult for Hercules.

TEKS 7

GO ON

Hercules. He looks harmless, but the maidens by the river warned me. I must hang on to him with a deadly grip until he
25 gives me the directions I need.

Narrator. So Hercules seized the fragile old man. Within seconds, the man began changing form. He became, in turn, a fierce stag, a screaming gull, a three-headed dog with razor-sharp teeth, a six-legged man-monster, and finally a
30 gigantic slithering snake! Throughout the transformations, Hercules never loosened his grip.

Hercules. It takes more than imaginary dangers to frighten me, Old Man. I know what you are beneath your shifting shapes.

35 **Old Man.** *(breathlessly)* All right. I surrender. Who are you, and what do you want from me?

Hercules. I am Hercules. You must tell me how to get to the garden of the Hesperides.

Old Man. Ah, Hercules, I have heard of your deeds. I am
40 honored to meet such a hero, and I will reveal to you what I know. Travel first south and then east as far as you can go. When you feel your next step will plunge you off the edge of the earth, then you will see the enormous giant, Atlas himself, who anchors the sky with his outstretched arms. He can tell
45 you how to obtain the apples.

Hercules. I am much obliged to you, Old Man. And, I apologize for handling you so harshly. I hope you bear me no ill will.

Narrator. With the Old Man's words of forgiveness echoing in
50 his ears, Hercules strode off, filled with renewed energy. Along the way, he battled and defeated the giant Antaeus. Then he had to cross the burning deserts in Africa. Finally, he came to an ocean so vast that he could not imagine how to navigate it. He looked and waited, refusing to admit defeat.
55 Straining his eyes, he saw a massive golden cup, perhaps the giant's goblet, bobbing over the waves. Crawling in, Hercules sailed along, washing up on the shore of a remote island.

CONNOTATION
Besides its literal meaning, a word may have connotations, or ideas and feelings that are associated with it. For example, the word *deeds* in line 39 means "actions or feats." In this context, however, the Old Man is remarking on the deeds of a hero. The word takes on the connotation of amazing acts of strength and bravery.

TEKS 1B

ARCHETYPE
An archetype is a model that is often found in Greek mythology. An archetype can be a plot, a character, an image, or a setting. Hercules is an archetypal hero; the hero's journey (lines 39–45) is also an archetype.

TEKS 2B, 4

GO ON

Hercules. *(stumbling unsteadily from the cup and gazing*
60 *upward with an expression of awe on his face)* I have
traveled for many lifetimes, it seems to me, but never have
I beheld such a sight. This giant upon whose mercy I must
throw myself is taller than the tallest mountain! His head
reaches into the clouds, and each of his eyes is as wide as
65 the Aegean Sea. His hands—each bigger than Greece
itself!—support the entire sky. Yet he looks downcast, weary,
and despairing, as if this weight is too much for him.

Atlas. *(looking down as the clouds move from his eyes)* Who
are you, my little man?

70 **Hercules.** O great one with a voice as loud as thunder, I am
Hercules. I seek the garden of the Hesperides.

Atlas. You do, do you? And what do you want with the
garden?

Hercules. I desire three of the golden apples for the king
75 whom I serve.

Atlas. I am the only one who can get those for you. But, as
you can see, I must support the sky. I'm afraid you have
come all this way for nothing.

Hercules. Please, those apples are worth much more to me
80 than the gold from which they are cast. Could you rest the
sky upon two mountain peaks while you help me?

Atlas. No. Nothing is high enough to allow me to slip out
from under this burden, or believe me, I would. You are
doomed to failure, I fear, unless . . .

85 **Hercules.** Yes?

Atlas. Unless you stand on the tallest summit and take the
sky on your own shoulders. But perhaps you are not strong
enough.

Hercules. I am Hercules. Of course I am strong enough!

90 **Atlas.** Then let us exchange, and I will be on my way.

Narrator. Hercules agreed quickly. He had sympathy for the
giant, tied to such a heavy responsibility. Deep in his heart,
he also wanted to boast that he had held up the sky. And, he

TRAGIC FLAW
Another common
archetype in literature is
the tragic flaw, a weakness
that can prevent a hero
from accomplishing his or
her goals. Readers often
must infer the hero's flaw
from the character's words
and actions. Hercules's
tragic flaw is revealed in
his discussion with Atlas in
lines 86–89. Think about
what that flaw is.

TEKS 2B, 4; Fig. 19B

GO ON

needed those apples. So, balancing the sky on his fingertips,
95 Atlas propped it on Hercules's back. Then, feeling relief for
the first time in centuries, Atlas frolicked about and roared
with laughter. He strode off without a backward glance.

Hercules. I am not sure that I made a wise decision. What if
Atlas does not return? Already, the sky grows oppressive. Yet
100 think of the consequences if it were to tilt or fall! Stars would
tumble down like confetti, and the sun's chariot could not
follow its path.

Narrator. Just then, a shadow passing over warned Hercules
that Atlas had returned.

105 **Hercules.** Dear fellow, I am so relieved to see you. What
magnificent apples, truly more like pumpkins. How can I ever
repay you for your kindness?

Atlas. Don't worry. You are repaying me. If you think the sky
is heavy now, wait until you have borne it a thousand years.

110 **Hercules.** What? Surely, you jest. I cannot support this
burden forever!

Atlas. But you have to, if I don't take it back.

Hercules. At least, let me make a cushion of my lion's skin to
protect my shoulders from becoming rubbed raw. Take the
115 sky for just a minute, if you would.

Atlas. Certainly. It is the least I can do in return for my
freedom.

Hercules. Thank you again for the apples. (*He snatches
them up and walks briskly offstage.*)

120 **Atlas.** Come back . . . You tricked me!

Narrator. With the desperate shouts of the giant pursuing
him, Hercules embarked on his journey home and delivered
the golden apples safely to the king. Now that his labor was
successfully done, it might seem that he had earned some
125 rest. But the Fates had other plans in store for Hercules.
Knowing that he could not avoid his destiny, Hercules soon
set off on another adventure.

ELEMENTS OF DRAMA
Notice that in lines
121–127, the narrator
reappears to end the story.
He tells what happened
at the end of Hercules's
journey and then points
out that Hercules will set
off on another journey. The
narrator's job in this play is
to fill in the missing details
so that the audience gets
a full account of what
happened.

TEKS 4

Name _____ Date _____

1 The italicized stage directions in this play tell all of the following except —

A what the characters do
B how the characters appear
C how the stage is lit
D what the scenery looks like

EXPLANATION: The stage directions tell about the characters and the lighting. **D** is correct. There are no stage directions that address scenery.
- **A** is incorrect. The direction in line 68 says that Atlas is looking down as the clouds move from his eyes.
- **B** is incorrect. At Hercules's first entrance, he appears "tall and muscle-bound with a proud bearing."
- **C** is incorrect. The first stage direction addresses lighting as the play opens.

TEKS 4

2 According to lines 13–18, Hercules's main goal in completing his journey is to achieve —

F heroic glory
G relief from guilt
H revenge for Hera's cruelty
J the rescue of an old man

EXPLANATION: Heroic journeys can be taken for many reasons. Hercules says that Hera caused him to lose his mind and kill his family, and that this journey is the only way he can relieve his guilt over that horrible crime. **G** is correct.
- **F** is incorrect. Hercules does not mention wanting to be a hero.
- **H** is incorrect. Although Hera caused his suffering, he does not say he wants to have revenge.
- **J** is incorrect. He is looking for the Old Man of the Sea, but not to rescue him.

TEKS 2B, 4; Fig. 19B

3 The first obstacle Hercules encounters on his heroic journey is —

A Hera
B the Old Man of the Sea
C a six-legged monster
D Atlas

EXPLANATION: The first obstacle is the Old Man of the Sea. **B** is correct. Hercules needs information from the Old Man, but the man transforms into many terrifying illusions before he admits defeat and gives the information.
- **A** is incorrect. Hera has caused problems for Hercules in the past, but she is not an obstacle in the quest.
- **C** is incorrect. The monster is one of the Old Man's shifting shapes.
- **D** is incorrect. Hercules encounters Atlas near the end of his journey.

TEKS 2B, 4

4 Atlas convinces Hercules to take the sky by appealing to his —

F kindness
G guilt
H greed
J pride

EXPLANATION: This part of the play reveals Hercules's pride. **J** is correct. Hercules agrees to take the sky after Atlas suggests Hercules is not strong enough to do so.
- **F** is incorrect because Hercules does not act out of kindness.
- **G** is incorrect. Hercules is motivated to fulfill the quest out of guilt, but this is not why he takes the sky.
- **H** is incorrect. It is not greed that motivates Hercules; he says he does not care about the apples' value in gold (lines 79–80).

TEKS 4; Fig. 19B

5 In Hercules's dialogue in lines 59–67, the playwright uses imagery—language that appeals to the senses—to describe and emphasize —

A Atlas's size
B Atlas's good looks
C Hercules's strength
D Hercules's exhaustion

EXPLANATION: The language describes the giant Atlas, whose "head reaches into the clouds" and whose eyes are each "as wide as the Aegean Sea." These images emphasize Atlas's enormous size. **A** is correct.
- **B** is incorrect. The language describes how big Atlas is, not how handsome.
- **C** is incorrect. Hercules is not describing his own strength in this dialogue.
- **D** is incorrect. Hercules does not describe his own fatigue; he says Atlas looks weary.

TEKS 7

6 The "sun's chariot" (line 101) is an allusion to the sun god Helios's chariot. This allusion suggests that ancient Greeks believed —

F the sun revolved around the moon
G the sun traveled across the sky in a chariot
H the gods made the sun out of a chariot
J each star was carried in its own chariot

EXPLANATION: In line 101, Hercules says the sun's chariot follows a path across the sky. **G** is correct. The ancient Greeks believed that Helios pulled the sun across the sky each day in a chariot.
- **F** is incorrect. The allusion to Helios's chariot does not have anything to do with the moon.
- **H** is incorrect. The phrase "the sun's chariot" suggests that the sun and the chariot are two separate things, not that the sun is a chariot.
- **J** is incorrect. Hercules does not suggest that the stars have chariots; instead of being unable to travel across the sky, the stars would simply fall down.

TEKS 7; Fig. 19B

7 Hercules is an archetypal hero—he is a model of strength and bravery. What event in the play's plot is a direct result of these heroic qualities?

A Hercules describes his intense guilt over the killing of his family and says he is willing to do anything to relieve his guilt.
B Hercules grabs the Old Man of the Sea and holds on tightly until he surrenders, even though the Old Man undergoes a series of terrifying transformations.
C Hercules comes to the edge of a vast sea and climbs into a golden cup that allows him to float to the shore of a remote island.
D Hercules feels panicked at the thought of taking on Atlas's burden forever and quickly devises a trick to get Atlas to take it back.

EXPLANATION: Grabbing the Old Man of the Sea and enduring the creature's frightening transformations is a bold act of bravery. Holding on tightly enough to force the creature's surrender requires the strength of a hero. **B** is correct.
- **A** is incorrect. Anyone would feel guilty after killing his or her family. Hercules's heroic qualities do not affect this event.
- **C** is incorrect. Climbing into the cup might require bravery because the outcome would be uncertain, but floating across the sea is a passive act that requires no heroic strength.
- **D** is incorrect. Hercules's trick requires cleverness and quick thinking, but not strength or bravery.

TEKS 2B, 4

8 Review the use of the word <u>snatches</u> in line 118. It literally means "grabs quickly." What connotation does the word have in the context of the surrounding dialogue?

F Hercules seizes the apples with triumphant glee.

G Hercules takes the apples reluctantly but firmly.

H Hercules quietly removes the apples and hopes that Atlas will not notice.

J Hercules grabs the apples impulsively but then feels uncertain what to do with them.

> **EXPLANATION:** In the dialogue surrounding line 118, Hercules tricks Atlas into taking the sky back. When he sees that his trick has worked, he snatches the apples and immediately leaves Atlas with his burden. He is thrilled that his trick has worked. **F** is correct.
> - **G** is incorrect. Hercules is desperate to get the apples, so there is no reluctance in his action.
> - **H** is incorrect. Hercules thanks Atlas for the apples, so he is not hoping to escape notice.
> - **J** is incorrect. Hercules leaves the scene immediately after snatching the apples; he knows he must take them to the king to complete his labor.

TEKS 1B; Fig. 19B

Answer the following question in the space provided.

---

9 Stories from Greek mythology often involve the struggle of a hero to overcome a tragic flaw. Describe Hercules's tragic flaw and the effect it has on events in the story. Does he overcome this flaw in the play, or will he likely have to deal with it in other quests?

EXPLANATION

Rubric, high-scoring response:

- Reflects a perceptive awareness of text meaning and complexities; makes meaningful connections across the text
- Uses specific, well-chosen evidence from the text, supporting validity of response
- Shows deep understanding of the text through ideas and supporting text evidence

Sample Response: Hercules's tragic flaw is his pride. Atlas exploits this flaw when he suggests that Hercules might not be strong enough to hold up the sky, to which Hercules replies, "I am Hercules. Of course I am strong enough!" He likes the idea that he will be able to boast later that he held up the sky, and so he take Atlas's burden just to prove he is strong enough to do it. However, this action has a larger importance because Hercules would not have been able to get the apples for the king and complete his quest if he hadn't taken the sky from Atlas temporarily. Hercules does not appear to overcome his pride in this story; he will probably make decisions based on pride in future adventures.

TEKS 2B, 4; Fig. 19A, 19B

© Houghton Mifflin Harcourt Publishing Company

STOP

Reading Informational Text: Expository Text

In this part of the book, you will read an informational article with instruction about the elements of expository text. Following the selection are sample questions and answers about the article. The purpose of this section is to show you how to understand and analyze expository text.

To begin, review the TEKS that relate to expository text:

EXPOSITORY TEXT TEKS	WHAT IT MEANS TO YOU
(9) Comprehension of Informational Text/Expository Text Students analyze, make inferences and draw conclusions about expository text and provide evidence from text to support their understanding. Students are expected to:	
(A) summarize text and distinguish between a summary and a critique and identify non-essential information in a summary and unsubstantiated opinions in a critique;	You will summarize expository texts. You will also tell the difference between a summary and a critique and identify unnecessary information in a summary and unsupported opinions in a critique.
(B) distinguish among different kinds of evidence (e.g., logical, empirical, anecdotal) used to support conclusions and arguments in texts;	You will make distinctions among different kinds of evidence, including logical, empirical, and anecdotal evidence, that an author uses to support arguments and conclusions in expository texts.
(C) make and defend subtle inferences and complex conclusions about the ideas in text and their organizational patterns; and	You will make inferences and conclusions about the ideas and the ways those ideas are organized in expository text and defend those inferences and conclusions with evidence from the text.
(D) synthesize and make logical connections between ideas and details in several texts selected to reflect a range of viewpoints on the same topic and support those findings with textual evidence.	You will synthesize and connect ideas and details from several expository texts having different perspectives on the same topic and support your findings with evidence from the texts.

The selection that follows provides instruction on the expository text TEKS as well as other TEKS. It also covers reading comprehension skills, such as summarizing and making inferences about text.

As you read the article "Where the Heart Is," notice the various kinds of evidence the author presents to support ideas and conclusions. The annotations in the margins will guide you as you read.

© Houghton Mifflin Harcourt Publishing Company

Guided Reading

Read this selection. Then answer the questions that follow.

Where the Heart Is

1   On a cold February evening in 1924, a gaunt dog limped up to a farmhouse in Silverton, Oregon, where he had once lived with his family as a pup. But the house was silent, the family long departed. Since August, the dog's lonely journey had taken him across Illinois and Iowa. He had swum rivers, including the dangerous and icy Missouri; he had crossed the great Rocky Mountains in the middle of winter. He had caught squirrels and rabbits for food. At times he had been helped by strangers: He had eaten stew with hobos and Thanksgiving dinner with a family who sheltered him for several weeks. But once he had regained his strength, the dog traveled on, always heading west. The dog lay down to rest for the night at the empty farmhouse. In the morning, on paws with pads worn almost to bone, he made his way slowly into town, into the restaurant building where his family now lived, and climbed upstairs to a bedroom, to lick the face of the man he had walked some three thousand miles to find. Bobby had come home.

2   Two-year-old Bobby, partly English sheepdog but mostly collie, had become separated from Frank Brazier while on vacation in Indiana. When word got out about Bobby's remarkable journey, the president of the Oregon Humane Society decided to document the facts and find the people who had seen or helped Bobby along the way. Bobby eventually became one of the most honored heroes in dog history, recognized with numerous medals and awards for his courage, devotion, and perseverance.

3   How did Bobby find his way home? Nobody knows for sure. We do know that Bobby's story is unusual but not unique. For centuries there have been reports of animals performing mystifying and wonderful feats like Bobby's. There are stories of other animals who tracked their families, sometimes over thousands of miles, to places where the animals themselves had never been, over routes the owners had never traveled. The story of Sugar may be the longest recorded trip of this kind.

MAKING INFERENCES
Making an inference means combining evidence from the text with your own knowledge to draw a conclusion. For example, using the details in the first two sentences of paragraph 1, you can infer that the dog was separated from his owner as a puppy and was not around when the family moved.

Fig. 19B

ANECDOTAL EVIDENCE
An anecdote is a brief story used to illustrate a point. In paragraph 3, the author states the conclusion that "Bobby's story is unusual but not unique." Then, in paragraph 4, the author provides anecdotal evidence to support this conclusion.

TEKS 9B

GO ON ➡

4   Stacy Woods, a high school principal, planned to move with her family from Anderson, California, to a farm in Gage, Oklahoma, 1,500 miles away. She couldn't take her cat Sugar, because he was terrified of riding in the car. So a neighbor agreed to adopt him. Fourteen months later, as Woods was milking a cow in her Oklahoma barn, Sugar jumped through an open window onto her shoulder. The astonished Woods family later learned that Sugar had disappeared three weeks after they had left him with the neighbor. Proving that the cat was really Sugar was easy because Sugar had an unusual hip deformity. But the main question remains unanswered today: How did Sugar find his owner? Similar questions have been raised about many other animals. How did Hugh Brady Perkins's homing pigeon find his way to Hugh's hospital window, 120 miles from his home, after the boy was rushed to the hospital in the middle of the night? How do some pets know when their favorite family members are coming home unexpectedly? How do some pets know from great distances when their family members are hurt or ill or in trouble?

5   In recent decades, researchers have studied questions like these. They have pondered the possibility that animals draw on information picked up in some way other than through the five well-known senses (sight, hearing, smell, taste, and touch).

6   Researchers have found that some animals have senses humans lack, like bats' ability to detect objects from echoes and certain snakes' ability to sense tiny temperature differences through special organs. Some people theorize that animals have a form of ESP (extrasensory perception). At Duke University, Joseph Banks Rhine collected more than five hundred stories of unexplainable animal feats that seem to support this theory. Rhine devoted his life to researching these events. Studies conducted at the Research Institute at Rockland State Hospital in New York also support the notion of an extrasensory connection between animals and humans, particularly humans the animals know well and trust.

7   Of course, whatever our theories say, we don't really know what goes on in the heart and mind of an animal. Perhaps the question of *how* they find us is not the most important one. A better question to ponder may be *why* they find us, even when faced with overwhelming difficulties. It has been said that home is where the heart is. It's clear that for Bobby and Sugar and countless others, home is where one particular heart is.

EMPIRICAL EVIDENCE
Empirical evidence is gathered from observation or experiments. In paragraph 6, the author uses empirical evidence, such as bats' ability to detect objects from echoes, to support the conclusion that animals use more than the five senses to gain information.

TEKS 9B

AUTHOR'S PURPOSE
Throughout the article, the author provides various kinds of evidence relating to animal behavior. In the last paragraph, she states her conclusion about what motivates animals to find their lost owners. Based on all of this information, you can infer the author's purpose, or reason for writing the article.

TEKS 8, 9C; Fig. 19B

GO ON

Use "Where the Heart Is" (pp. 35–36) to answer questions 1–6.

1 Which detail from the selection supports the inference that what Bobby did was unusual?

A The actions of the president of the Oregon Humane Society

B The story of a cat finding its way home

C The information about bats detecting objects from echoes

D The story about Hugh Brady Perkins's homing pigeon

EXPLANATION: The president of the Oregon Humane Society documented the facts of Bobby's story. If the dog's journey had been commonplace, no one would have bothered to research the story. Therefore, **A** is correct.
- **B** and **D** are incorrect. These stories show that other animals have done what Bobby did, making his journey seem less unusual.
- **C** is incorrect. The information about bats does not relate to Bobby's story, which is about a pet finding its way home.

TEKS 9C; Fig. 19B

2 The details that the author includes support the inference that she is —

F a scientist who has researched animals

G an animal lover fascinated by the stories

H a cynic who is suspicious of the stories

J a reporter investigating whether Frank Brazier is telling the truth

EXPLANATION: The author's use of words such as "courage," "devotion," "mystifying," and "wonderful" (paragraphs 2–3) suggest that she is fascinated by the stories. **G** is correct.
- **F** is incorrect. No details in the text suggest that the author is a scientist.
- **H** is incorrect. If she were suspicious of the stories, she would probably quote experts who also doubt them.
- **J** is incorrect. The author does not question Brazier's story.

TEKS 9C; Fig. 19B

3 In paragraph 4, Stacy Woods uses empirical evidence to —

A find her lost cat, Sugar

B prove that the cat in Oklahoma is Sugar

C persuade her neighbor to take the cat

D prove that all cats can do what Sugar did

EXPLANATION: Empirical evidence is based on direct observation. **B** is correct. Woods observes that the cat in Oklahoma has an unusual hip deformity, proving that the cat is Sugar.
- **A** is incorrect. She does not look for the cat; the cat finds her.
- **C** is incorrect. The text does not say how she convinces her neighbor to take the cat.
- **D** is incorrect. Woods does not attempt to prove this. She only observes what Sugar does.

TEKS 9B

GO ON

4 Joseph Banks Rhine (paragraph 6) supported his theory using —

F   empirical evidence, because he observed something firsthand

G   empirical evidence, because he conducted experiments

H   anecdotal evidence, because he collected stories

J   logical evidence, because he relied entirely on reasoning

> **EXPLANATION:** Rhine collected stories, or anecdotes, about animals and used them to support the conclusion that animals have a form of ESP. **H** is correct.
> - **F** and **G** are incorrect. Rhine did not observe the animals or conduct experiments.
> - **J** is incorrect. Although Rhine probably used reasoning to draw a conclusion, the anecdotes he collected are the most important evidence for his theory.

TEKS 9B

5 The Latin prefix *extra-* means "outside" or "beyond." Knowing the meaning of this prefix helps you infer that the word <u>extrasensory</u> in paragraph 6 means —

A   not making sense

B   outside the natural world

C   included in the five senses

D   beyond the ordinary senses

> **EXPLANATION:** Paragraphs 5 and 6 discuss how animals gather information in ways other than through the five well-known senses. *Extrasensory* means "beyond the ordinary senses." **D** is correct.
> - **A** is incorrect. The context in which the word appears tells you that it involves sensory perception, not logical sense.
> - **B** is incorrect. The word is used in the context of scientific research about the natural world.
> - **C** is incorrect because the prefix *extra-* means the opposite of "included in."

TEKS 1A

6 What is the author's purpose for writing this selection?

F   To inform readers about a topic that she finds interesting and mysterious

G   To persuade people to keep track of their pets so they do not become lost

H   To entertain readers with anecdotes about funny animal behaviors

J   To explain the latest methods for finding lost pets

> **EXPLANATION:** The author shares various kinds of evidence to support the idea that animals have abilities that cannot be explained in terms of the five senses. The concluding paragraph states that people do not fully understand "what goes on in the heart and mind of an animal." The author clearly finds the topic both interesting and mysterious. **F** is correct.
> - **G** and **J** are incorrect. The author shares several stories about lost pets but does not argue that people should make more of an effort to keep track of their pets or explain any methods for finding lost pets.
> - **H** is incorrect. The anecdotes about lost pets finding their owners are fascinating and touching, but not funny. Also, the author uses these anecdotes to support conclusions about animal behavior. They are not intended merely as entertainment.

TEKS 8, 9C

Answer the following question in the space provided.

---

7 Sum up the scientific explanation about the deep connection some animals have to their owners, and explain why you agree or disagree with the theory. Use evidence from the selection to support your ideas.

EXPLANATION

Rubric, high-scoring response:

- Reflects a perceptive awareness of text meaning and complexities; makes meaningful connections across the text
- Uses specific, well-chosen evidence from the text, supporting validity of response
- Shows deep understanding of the text through ideas and supporting text evidence

Sample Response: The scientific explanation in the article is that animals have extrasensory perception, or the ability to get information through senses other than the "big five": sight, hearing, smell, touch, and taste. Based on the information in the article, I don't agree with this theory. Two of the examples given—bats using sounds to locate objects and snakes sensing temperature differences—point to supersensory, not extrasensory, perception. Bats simply have intense powers of hearing, and snakes are intensely sensitive to touch. Furthermore, these examples don't explain dogs' abilities to find their owners from great distances. Another common sense—a sense of direction—and dogs' well-established sense of smell might just as easily explain these feats.

TEKS 9A, 9C; Fig. 19A, 19B

STOP

Reading Informational Text: Persuasive Text

In this part of the book, you will read a persuasive essay with instruction about the elements of persuasive text. Following the selection are sample questions and answers about the essay. The purpose of this section is to show you how to understand and analyze persuasive text.

To begin, review the TEKS that relate to persuasive text:

PERSUASIVE TEXT TEKS	WHAT IT MEANS TO YOU
(10) Comprehension of Informational Text/Persuasive Text Students analyze, make inferences and draw conclusions about persuasive text and provide evidence from text to support their analysis. Students are expected to:	
(A) explain shifts in perspective in arguments about the same topic and evaluate the accuracy of the evidence used to support the different viewpoints within those arguments; and	You will discuss changes in perspective in arguments about the same topic and evaluate how well authors use evidence to support those different perspectives.
(B) analyze contemporary political debates for such rhetorical and logical fallacies as appeals to commonly held opinions, false dilemmas, appeals to pity, and personal attacks.	You will analyze the use of rhetorical and logical fallacies, such as appeals to commonly held opinions, false dilemmas, appeals to pity, and personal attacks, in contemporary political debates.

The selection that follows provides instruction on the persuasive text TEKS as well as other TEKS. It also covers reading comprehension skills, such as making inferences about text.

As you read the essay "To Build or Not to Build," identify the writer's main claim and the evidence used to support it. The annotations in the margins will guide you as you read.

© Houghton Mifflin Harcourt Publishing Company

Guided Reading

Read this selection. Then answer the questions that follow.

To Build or Not to Build

1   It's a beautiful spring morning at Millers Woods. The sun is shining brightly and birds are chirping. Some fifth-graders from a nearby elementary school are walking one of the nature trails with their teacher, identifying the various wildflowers they see and eagerly watching for any signs of animal life.

2   In a neighborhood on the other side of the city, the sun is shining but the mood is anything but cheerful. People sit idly on their front porches. Some have been unemployed for as long as two years, having lost their jobs in the first wave of layoffs at the auto plant. Others have been out of work since January, when the plant closed permanently. All of them wonder what the future will hold. Will they be able to stay in their homes or send their children to college? Will there even be enough money to keep food on the table?

3   A proposal to build a new municipal airport on the land that is now Millers Woods pits the interests of schoolchildren and unemployed workers—as well as other groups—against one another. On one side are those who favor construction of the airport. On the other side are those who want to preserve Millers Woods.

4   Concerned citizens who favor construction of the airport point to our city's 20% rate of unemployment. They note that building the airport would keep construction workers in our city busy for more than a year and would provide at least 200 permanent new jobs for city residents. According to a study done by the <u>chamber</u> of commerce, a new airport would help make our city more attractive for tourism and as a convention center. An increase in the tourist and convention trade would bring more business to local hotels, restaurants, and retail stores. It would also create new jobs.

OPPOSING VIEWPOINTS
This essay concerns a proposal to build an airport on a wooded area. In paragraphs 1–5, the writer lays out the claims, or arguments, on both sides of the issue. Each argument is supported with reasons and evidence. For example, a reason for not building the airport on Millers Woods is that elementary school children benefit from being able to study nature there (paragraph 1). Continue reading to find the evidence for the opposing argument.

TEKS 10A

EVIDENCE
Evidence to support an argument may include specific facts, examples, or quotations. In paragraph 4, the writer cites the city's 20% unemployment rate as a reason for building the airport because the project would create at least 200 new jobs.

TEKS 10A

GO ON

5   Residents who want to preserve Millers Woods emphasize its value as an educational and recreational resource. Each year, thousands of people visit the area to hike, picnic, and observe its abundant plant and animal life. If an airport is built on the site, the habitat of many animals native to our region will be destroyed. Opponents of the airport also point out that the levels of noise and air pollution in our city will increase substantially if a new airport is built.

6   Underlying the debate are two different sets of priorities for our city. Should we place the highest priority on woodpeckers and trees, or should we extend a helping hand to our neighbors who are struggling? Do aesthetic and environmental concerns take priority over the economic well-being of a large segment of our community, or vice versa? There is no doubt that if the airport is built, our city will lose a valuable natural resource, and the habitat of many animals will be destroyed. In addition, we will have to deal with noise and air pollution. But these consequences must be weighed against the problem of chronic unemployment and underemployment for many of our city's residents. Their homes and lives are no less at risk than those of the woodland animals.

7   Most people agree that when times are tough, we must look out for our own. Protecting a woodland preserve is a lofty ideal, but the interests of our fellow human beings must trump those of squirrels and flowers. This means supporting airport construction at Millers Woods. Every effort to find a suitable alternative to building on the Millers Woods site has failed. We have a pressing need to reduce local unemployment and to promote economic growth—both of which the construction of an airport will achieve. At least for the short run, we must act on behalf of people's well-being.

FALLACY
A fallacy is an error in logic. Paragraph 6 illustrates the fallacy called a false dilemma. The author implies there are only two choices: build or do not build, have the woodland destroyed or have people suffer the hardships of unemployment. Other options, such as creating a new woodland or building another facility that could employ people, are not discussed.

TEKS 10B

CLAIM
In paragraph 7, the writer states his claim, or position, on the issue. He argues that readers should support airport construction at Millers Woods because there is a pressing need to reduce local unemployment and to promote economic growth. Note that the claim is not stated in a single sentence.

TEKS 10; Fig. 19B

GO ON

Use **"To Build or Not to Build"** (pp. 41–42) to answer questions 1–6.

1 Read the following sentence from the selection.

> *Most people agree that when times are tough, we must look out for our own.*

What logical fallacy is illustrated in the sentence?

A False dilemma
B Appeal to commonly held opinion
C Appeal to pity
D Personal attack

EXPLANATION: This question asks you to make an inference about which error in logic the writer has made. An appeal to commonly held opinion incorrectly assumes that something must be true because most people believe it to be true. **B** is correct. The statement begins, "Most people agree that . . ."
- **A** is incorrect. A false dilemma suggests that only two options are available. The statement does not describe any options.
- **C** is incorrect. An appeal to pity seeks to create a feeling of sympathy as a way to get agreement with a certain viewpoint. The statement does not seek to create a feeling of sympathy.
- **D** is incorrect. The statement does not attack or insult any person.

TEKS 10B; Fig. 19B

2 Which sentence from the selection gives a reason to support building a new municipal airport at Millers Woods?

F *In a neighborhood on the other side of the city, the sun is shining but the mood is anything but cheerful.*

G *According to a study done by the chamber of commerce, a new airport would help make our city more attractive for tourism and as a convention center.*

H *Each year, thousands of people visit the area to hike, picnic, and observe its abundant plant and animal life.*

J *At least for the short run, we must act on behalf of people's well-being.*

EXPLANATION: The question asks you to identify a reason that supports the argument in favor of building the airport. **G** is correct because it points out a benefit of the airport.
- **F** is incorrect because it does not concretely state a reason or fact that supports the proposal to build an airport.
- **H** is incorrect because it states a reason to oppose building the airport and support the preservation of Millers Woods.
- **J** is incorrect because it is a restatement of the author's claim that the airport should be built. It does not include a reason.

TEKS 10A

3 Which paragraph most clearly summarizes the two opposing arguments on the airport issue?

A Paragraph 1
B Paragraph 3
C Paragraph 5
D Paragraph 7

EXPLANATION: Review each paragraph before answering the question. **B** is correct because paragraph 3 directly states the two opposing arguments using the phrases "On one side" and "On the other side."
- **A** and **C** are incorrect because the details in each of these paragraphs relate to just one argument.
- **D** is incorrect because paragraph 7 focuses on the writer's position on the issue and does not give equal attention to the two arguments.

TEKS 10A; Fig. 19B

4 Read the following dictionary entry.

chamber \chām´ bər\ *n.* **1.** a bedroom **2.** a board or council **3.** a place where funds are held; a treasury **4.** an enclosed space in the body of a living thing

What is the definition of chamber as it is used in paragraph 4?

F Definition 1
G Definition 2
H Definition 3
J Definition 4

EXPLANATION: Paragraph 4 identifies the chamber of commerce as an entity that has conducted a study. It is a group of people concerned with commerce, or trade. **G** is correct because a board or council is a group of people who meet to discuss common concerns. **F, H,** and **J** are incorrect because none of these things could conduct a study.

TEKS 1E

5 According to the author of the selection, the main reason to support building the airport is that it will —

A cause noise and air pollution
B create many new jobs
C cause rehiring at the city's auto plant
D bring about 0% unemployment

EXPLANATION: This question asks you to identify the main support for the author's claim, or position. **B** is correct because paragraphs 4 and 6 focus on reducing unemployment as a benefit of building the airport.
- **A** is incorrect because noise and air pollution are reasons to oppose building the airport.
- **C** is incorrect because the new jobs the writer cites will not come from the auto plant.
- **D** is incorrect. The writer asserts that the airport will help address unemployment but does not state that it will reduce unemployment to zero.

TEKS 10

6 In paragraph 7, the context suggests that a good synonym for the word trump is —

F kill
G serve
H treat
J override

EXPLANATION: To answer this question, review the context in which the word *trump* appears. **J** is correct because the reader by now knows that the writer is in favor of replacing the woodland with an airport, so "the interests of our fellow human beings" override "those of squirrels and flowers."
- **F** is incorrect. The meaning of *kill* is too extreme to fit the context sentence.
- **G** is incorrect. If substituted in the sentence, *serve* conveys an idea that is the opposite of the writer's view.
- **H** is incorrect. The word *treat* does not fit the meaning of the context sentence.

TEKS 1B

Answer the following question in the space provided.

---

7 Do you think the writer's argument in "To Build or Not to Build" is effective? Support your answer with evidence from the selection.

EXPLANATION

Rubric, high-scoring response:

- Reflects a perceptive awareness of text meaning and complexities; makes meaningful connections across the text
- Uses specific, well-chosen evidence from the text, supporting validity of response
- Shows deep understanding of the text through ideas and supporting text evidence

Sample Response: In "To Build or Not to Build," the author declares his support for a proposal to build a new city airport at Millers Woods. I find his argument unconvincing. While the author provides strong evidence in support of his claim—the 20% rate of unemployment, including recent layoffs at the auto plant, and the fact that 200 permanent jobs will be created by the airport construction—he doesn't deal thoroughly with the opposing claim. Instead, the writer creates a false dilemma between preserving the woods and building an airport. He doesn't explain why the airport couldn't be built elsewhere, or why another, less environmentally destructive use couldn't be made of the woods. He also makes it sound as if building the airport equals caring for our citizens, when others can reasonably argue that preserving the citizens' environment is another way of caring.

TEKS 10A, 10B; Fig. 19A

Reading Literary Text: Paired Selections

In this part of the book, you will read two selections: a letter with instruction about the elements of literary nonfiction, and a short story with instruction about the elements of fiction. Following the selections are sample questions and answers about the two pieces. The purpose of this section is to show you how to understand and analyze selections from two different genres and how to compare and contrast them.

To begin, review the TEKS that relate to literary nonfiction and fiction:

LITERARY NONFICTION TEKS	WHAT IT MEANS TO YOU
(6) Comprehension of Literary Text/Literary Nonfiction Students understand, make inferences and draw conclusions about the varied structural patterns and features of literary nonfiction and provide evidence from text to support their understanding. Students are expected to evaluate the role of syntax and diction and the effect of voice, tone, and imagery on a speech, literary essay, or other forms of literary nonfiction.	You will understand and draw conclusions about the structure and elements of literary nonfiction and back up your analysis using examples from the text. You will also evaluate how an author's sentence structure, word choice, voice, tone, and use of imagery affect the message of a speech, literary essay, or other nonfiction work.

FICTION TEKS	WHAT IT MEANS TO YOU
(5) Comprehension of Literary Text/Fiction Students understand, make inferences and draw conclusions about the structure and elements of fiction and provide evidence from text to support their understanding. Students are expected to:	
(A) analyze isolated scenes and their contribution to the success of the plot as a whole in a variety of works of fiction;	You will examine specific scenes in fictional works and analyze how successfully those scenes advance the plot.
(B) analyze differences in the characters' moral dilemmas in works of fiction across different countries or cultures;	You will analyze the different ways characters respond to moral dilemmas in works of fiction from different countries and cultures.
(C) evaluate the connection between forms of narration (e.g., unreliable, omniscient) and tone in works of fiction; and	You will evaluate how the author's choice of a narrator affects the tone of works of fiction.
(D) demonstrate familiarity with works by authors from non-English-speaking literary traditions with emphasis on 20th century world literature.	You will become familiar with works by authors who come from peoples whose first language is not English, especially those from the 20th century.

The selections that follow provide instruction on the literary nonfiction TEKS, the fiction TEKS, and other TEKS. They also cover reading comprehension skills, such as summarizing and making inferences about text.

As you read the letter "How to Become a Writer" and the story "For the Love of the Dance," notice how the authors use the elements described in the charts above. Notice also the similarities and differences in structure and meaning between the letter and the story. The annotations in the margins will guide you as you read.

© Houghton Mifflin Harcourt Publishing Company

Name _____ Date _____

Guided Reading

Read the next two selections. Then answer the questions that follow.

from How to Become a Writer

by Helen Keller

Helen Keller lost her sight and hearing in 1882 when she was a baby. When she was six years old, she learned to communicate through sign language. She later learned to read and write using the Braille system. Keller became famous as a writer after her autobiography, The Story of My Life, *was published in 1903. She wrote the following letter to a blind boy in 1910.*

1   Your letter interested me very much, and I would gladly tell you how to become a writer if I knew. But alas! I do not know how to become one myself. No one can be taught to write. One can learn to write if he has it in him; but he does not learn from a teacher, counsellor, or adviser. No education, however careful and wise, will furnish talent. It only gives material to one who has talent to work with. If I could explain the process and command the secrets of this strange elusive faculty, the first thing I should do would be to write the greatest novel of the century, an epic and a volume of sonnets thrown in. I should at once set about making great writers of some hundreds and thousands of Americans. I should "stump" the States[1] and get bills passed for the promotion of high-grade literature. I should see to it that among our national products authors with noble powers had the chief place.

2   I believe the only place to look for the information you desire is in the biographies of successful authors. As far as I know, one fact is common to them all. In their youth they read good books and began writing in a simple way. They kept the best models of style before them. They played with words until they could criticise their own compositions and strike out dull or badly managed passages. They journeyed on, now taking a step forward, impelled by the desire to write, now at a standstill, held back by defects of style or lack of ideas. One day they wrote a real book, they awoke to find that

---

DICTION

A writer's diction, or choice of words, conveys a certain tone or attitude toward the subject and the reader. In paragraph 1, note how the highlighted phrases and sentences create a formal yet friendly tone.

TEKS 6; Fig. 19B

SYNTAX

Syntax is the order in which words are arranged in sentences. Note the inverted, or reversed, syntax of the last sentence in paragraph 1, which contributes to the formal tone of the letter. A more informal syntax is "I should see to it that authors with noble powers had the chief place among our national products."

TEKS 6

---

1. **"stump" the States:** travel around the United States making speeches to gain support for a proposal.

 GO ON

they had a literary gift—the idea had come, and they were prepared to express it! I would suggest that you read the autobiographies of Benjamin Franklin and Anthony Trollope. In these books the authors tell us, not how they learned to write—that was a thing not in their power to divulge—but what steps they took to improve their powers. And simple steps they are, such as you and I can follow. . . .

3   You see, there is but one road to authorship. It remains forever a way in which each man must go a-pioneering. The struggles of the pen may be as severe as those of the axe and hammer. One needs right mental eyes to discern the signs of talent which writers have left on their pages, like so many "blazes" upon trees in the forest. Well! I am not a novelist or a poet, I fear, and that metaphor is running away with me. What I mean is, we can follow where literary folk have gone; but, in order to be authors ourselves, to be followed, we must strike into a path where no one has preceded us. Before we publish anything, or set ourselves up as writers, we may imitate and even copy to our hearts' content, and when the time comes for us to send forth a message to the world, we shall have learned how to say it.

4   From your letter I judge that you do not read with your fingers.[2] You can do this, and you ought to learn as soon as possible. You are indeed fortunate that your parents can read aloud to you. But there is danger in only hearing language, and never seeing or touching it. Your memory will do you all the more service if you have embossed words placed at your finger-ends. Then reading for yourself will give you a better sense of language, and a good sense of words is the very basis of style.

IMAGERY
Imagery is the use of words and phrases to create a vivid picture in the reader's mind. In the extended metaphor in paragraph 3, Keller compares a struggling writer learning from the "best models of style" to someone navigating through a forest by following the blazes (path-finding marks) left on trees by an earlier pioneer.

TEKS 6; Fig. 19A

SUMMARIZING
At the end of paragraph 3, Keller sums up her explanation of the steps great writers like Franklin and Trollope must have taken in developing their talent. When you finish reading Keller's letter, think about how you would summarize it.

Fig. 19A

2. **read with your fingers:** Keller refers to the Braille system, in which patterns of embossed (raised) bumps represent letters that a blind person can read with his or her fingertips.

GO ON

For the Love of the Dance

In this fictional story, two young people are assigned to be partners in a dance competition. It's obvious that one of them has the talent to win the trophy. It's less clear what the other one has to offer.

1   The boy looked as if he would topple over in a stiff breeze. He was as tall and thin as a piece of angel-hair pasta, the kind that gets stuck between your back teeth because it's so skinny. As he shambled across the floor, loose-limbed and uncomfortable in his skin, his assigned partner sighed. She really didn't want to dance with him in the competition. She wanted a trophy. Unfortunately, she had no choice.

2   "Let's get started," said the instructor. "We'll run through the standard dances to see which one works best for the two of you together. Then, later in the month, we'll spend some time on your original routine."

3   The boy, soft-spoken, introduced himself to the girl. He said that he had never danced in public before, though he had watched a lot of dance shows to see what he could learn. Sheepishly, he also admitted that he had made up several dances on his own. The girl, barely able to hear him above the music, forced a grin and said she was sure that he would be fine.

4   He wasn't. He waltzed like a turkey vulture about to take off. His knees sagged, his arms flapped like wings, and his head bobbed as if on a spring. "Maybe the jitterbug is more your style," encouraged the instructor. The boy threw himself into the dance, heaving the girl a few feet into the air with a loud grunt, only to let her crumple to the floor. "Perhaps we will try the tango next," the instructor said. The boy, holding the girl's hands in his, extended his arms with a sweeping flourish. The girl's shoulders cracked. With his huge strides, he dragged her behind him like roadkill stuck to a car. As a last resort, they tried hip-hop. The boy appeared to be having a seizure.

NARRATOR
You can infer that the narrator of this story is not a character but an outside voice because the narrator refers to the boy, the girl, and the instructor in the third person. The point of view is third-person omniscient because the narrator can see into the minds of all the characters. Think about how the author uses this form of narration to reveal a particular tone, or attitude, toward the characters.

TEKS 5C; Fig. 19B

PLOT
Different scenes in which the characters interact move the plot along. The first dance rehearsal establishes key character traits that will affect later events. In paragraph 3, readers learn that the boy speaks softly, is interested in dance, and has made up dances. When he dances with the girl, however, he is extremely awkward (paragraph 4).

TEKS 5A

GO ON

5   "All right. We need a break," breathed the instructor tensely. Turning his head, he murmured to the girl, "We could appeal the rules and try to find you someone else. You have the ability to win the prize this year." About to agree, she glanced over. The boy was tapping his feet in time to the music with a huge smile on his face.

6   "Thanks," she said. "I don't know why, but I guess I'll stay with him."

7   Over the next few weeks, the boy grew less marionette-like, although he still displayed the odd convulsive tremor at times. The pair rejected the waltz, vetoed the tango, and decided to concentrate on the foxtrot for their first set piece. The instructor felt that the faster pace would disguise the boy's lack of coordination.

8   Not that the boy was worried. In his shy conversations with the girl, he confided how much he looked forward to the original part of the program. He loved doing the foxtrot, but in his spare time, he had been working on a dance that he thought would be perfect for the two of them. The girl shuddered, wondering why she had agreed to keep him as a partner and dreading how humiliated she would feel at the competition. The instructor, hoping he might be able to help, told the boy to bring in his music. It was time to get started on the new dance.

9   The next day the boy reverently handed his CD to the instructor. Then he explained where he got the idea for the dance. He said that his mom and dad owned a bakery. From the time he was a child, he had been fascinated by the transformation that occurred when all the separate ingredients—flour and sugar, eggs and butter—merged to become part of something new. That was his inspiration. He wanted his dance to be a metaphor for the process of creation. Then the boy offered to dance his part for them.

CONFLICT
The conversation between the instructor and the girl in paragraphs 5 and 6 highlights the story's conflict, or main problem. The girl must decide whether to continue dancing with the boy.

TEKS 5B

FORESHADOWING
Foreshadowing is a technique in which the author hints about something that will occur later in the story. In paragraph 8, the girl feels dread about the original dance the boy is working on, knowing they will have to perform it together. This creates a feeling of suspense as readers wonder how it will actually turn out.

TEKS 5A

GO ON

10   The music coming from the CD player was surprisingly haunting. As the melody wove its spell over the pair, the boy too was transformed. The ugly duckling became a graceful, beautiful swan. The boy brought his choreography to life: precise patterns alternated with sweeping gestures, telling a story through movements and sound. The girl stood there transfixed. Could this confident, controlled dancer possibly be the same <u>inept</u> partner she had propped up and dragged along for weeks? In the corner, the instructor stared, his mouth open. All the teaching in the world couldn't produce this kind of talent.

11   The dance ended; the boy blushed and grinned as the two spectators clapped and cheered. He said, "I know you're kind of astonished that I can do this. So am I. But I felt this dance grow inside of me. I knew it was right."

12   It would be nice to report that the boy and girl went on to win the competition. They did not. In fact, they didn't come close. The boy never really mastered the fox trot; it was someone else's dance, not his. Their hip-hop number was equally forgettable. However, they did impress the judges with their original performance, getting top marks in that category. As it turned out, the girl didn't mind losing. She wasn't even disappointed about the trophy. She felt different about dancing. Before, a dance was something she did with her arms, legs, and torso. Now it was something she became. She and the boy didn't stay dance partners, but he was happy to choreograph her routines after she found a new partner. And the boy—well, he still appeared tall and thin and awkward, except when he was dancing to the beat of his own drummer.

THEME
A theme is a message about life or human nature that the author wants readers to understand. The theme of this story is implied in paragraph 10, in the description of how well the boy dances when he is performing to his own music and choreography. Think about how the theme of the story might be similar to the theme of Helen Keller's letter.

TEKS 2A; Fig. 19B

GO ON ➔

Use "How to Become a Writer" (pp. 47–48) to answer questions 1–4.

1 Read the diagram below, which outlines the steps to becoming a good writer.

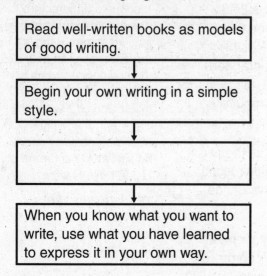

Read well-written books as models of good writing.

↓

Begin your own writing in a simple style.

↓

↓

When you know what you want to write, use what you have learned to express it in your own way.

According to Keller, which step belongs in the third box?

A Increase the complexity of your writing until it perfectly matches the style of the writers you admire.

B Practice writing until you can tell what you have done well or poorly and can edit your own work.

C Find a mentor who can teach you how to write more creatively.

D Read the biographies of famous writers and then follow in their footsteps.

EXPLANATION: Keller discusses the steps to becoming a writer in paragraph 2. She says that writers like Franklin and Trollope, after reading good books and starting to write simply, "played with words until they could criticise their own compositions and strike out dull or badly managed passages." **B** is correct because it paraphrases this idea.

• **A** and **D** are incorrect because Keller stresses the importance of developing one's own style, not imitating the work of others.

• **C** is incorrect because Keller says, "No one can be taught to write."

Fig. 19B

2 Which of these sentences from the letter uses imagery?

F *They journeyed on, now taking a step forward, impelled by the desire to write, now at a standstill, held back by defects of style or lack of ideas.*

G *One can learn to write if he has it in him; but he does not learn from a teacher, counsellor, or adviser.*

H *I should see to it that among our national products authors with noble powers had the chief place.*

J *From your letter I judge that you do not read with your fingers.*

EXPLANATION: In paragraph 2, aspiring writers are presented as being on a journey, taking steps forward (making progress) but also standing still (becoming stuck) at times. The imagery appeals to the senses of sight and touch. **F** is correct. **G, H,** and **J** are incorrect because they do not include sensory details that create strong images.

TEKS 6; Fig. 19A

3 In paragraph 3, the author's shift to using the pronoun *we* suggests that she —

A feels superior to the reader because of her experience

B identifies with the struggles of a would-be writer

C considers herself to be a successful author

D identifies with blind people who are learning to read

> **EXPLANATION:** This question asks you to evaluate the author's diction, or word choices. **B** is correct. Keller is addressing a blind boy who wrote to her about how to become a writer.
> - **A** is incorrect. Statements throughout the letter suggest Keller is modest about her own abilities.
> - **C** is incorrect. She names Franklin and Trollope as successful writers but not herself.
> - **D** is incorrect. Until the last paragraph, Keller addresses the subject of writing, not reading.

TEKS 6; Fig. 19B

4 Which of the following is the best summary of the selection?

F Helen Keller has received a letter from a blind boy about how to become a writer. She says that she would love to tell him the secret, but she does not know it herself. Good writing cannot be taught. Each writer must develop a unique style.

G Helen Keller recommends the autobiographies of Benjamin Franklin and Anthony Trollope to anyone who wants to learn how to become a writer. However, she fails to make a compelling argument against the idea that talent is the most important factor in becoming a great writer.

H Helen Keller explains that good writing is the product of years of practice. For someone who is blind, she emphasizes the importance of learning to read Braille. She says that hearing a book read aloud is not the same as reading it oneself. Reading text also gives a person a better sense of language, and "a good sense of words is the very basis of style."

J Helen Keller says that good writing cannot be taught. However, she explains this strategy: Read good books. Practice writing until you know when you've written something good. Then, when you know what you want to write, you will have the skills to express it in your own way. She also recommends that blind people learn to read Braille to develop a good sense of language.

> **EXPLANATION:** A good summary includes a text's main ideas and most important details. It does not express opinions about the text. **J** is correct because it accurately summarizes the key ideas from the entire letter.
> - **F** is incorrect because it leaves out important details about the process of developing a unique style.
> - **G** is incorrect. The references to Benjamin Franklin and Anthony Trollope are minor details. Also, this statement ends with an opinion about the selection.
> - **H** is incorrect because it focuses on the content of paragraph 4 but does not provide enough details from the rest of the selection.

TEKS 6; Fig. 19A

GO ON

Use "For the Love of the Dance" (pp. 49–51) to answer questions 5–9.

5 The main conflict in the story concerns —

 A the boy's ability to dance

 B the girl's lack of appreciation for the boy's choreography

 C the instructor's wish to help the boy

 D the boy's lack of interest in dancing

EXPLANATION: A conflict or struggle involving the main characters drives the plot of most stories. **A** is correct. The boy's poor dancing during practices causes frustration for his partner and the instructor and raises the question of whether the girl will decide to get another partner in order to win a trophy.
- **B** is incorrect. When the girl sees the boy's original dance, she is amazed at his talent and creativity.
- **C** is incorrect. The instructor is a minor character, and his desire to help the boy does not create a problem.
- **D** is incorrect. Details about the boy, such as his watching a lot of dance shows and making up several dances, show he is interested in dance.

TEKS 5B

6 Which excerpt from the story foreshadows a future development in the plot?

 F *The pair rejected the waltz, vetoed the tango, and decided to concentrate on the foxtrot for their first set piece.*

 G *In his shy conversations with the girl, he confided how much he looked forward to the original part of the program.*

 H *As it turned out, the girl didn't mind losing. She wasn't even disappointed about the trophy.*

 J *The dance ended; the boy blushed and grinned as the two spectators clapped and cheered.*

EXPLANATION: This question is about foreshadowing. The fact that the boy is looking forward to the original part of the program hints that something special or surprising may happen when he performs it. **G** is correct.
- **F** and **J** are incorrect because neither of these excerpts makes the reader wonder what will happen next.
- **H** is incorrect because it refers to an event at the very end of the story.

TEKS 5A

7 The scene in which the boy performs his own dance is important to the plot because —

A it confirms that the girl and the instructor have judged the boy accurately

B it is a turning point that points toward the resolution of the conflict

C it makes readers wonder how the boy learned to dance so well

D it resolves the story's main conflict

> **EXPLANATION:** The plot of a story usually involves a conflict that the characters must resolve. In this story, the main characters want to win a dance competition, but one partner (the boy) shows little dance ability. However, when he performs his original dance, he is transformed into a "graceful, beautiful swan."
> **B** is correct because this is a turning point in the plot. If the boy can dance this well in an original dance, he and the girl may have a chance in the competition.
> - **A** is incorrect. If anything, the boy's original dance shows that the girl and the instructor judged him too harshly.
> - **C** is incorrect because how the boy learned to dance is not crucial to the story's plot.
> - **D** is incorrect. The boy's surprisingly good original dance at the rehearsal is only the beginning of a resolution. The boy and girl still must dance in the competition.

TEKS 5A, 5B

8 In paragraph 10, the word <u>inept</u> means —

F skillful

G inappropriate

H inspired

J clumsy

> **EXPLANATION:** Reread paragraph 10 to see the context for *inept*. Note the contrast between *inept* and the words *graceful, confident,* and *controlled*. **J** is correct because *clumsy* also contrasts with *graceful, confident,* and *controlled*.
> - **F** is incorrect. *Skillful* is similar in meaning to *graceful, confident,* and *controlled,* but the context suggests that *inept* has an opposite meaning.
> - **G** is incorrect, because while *inept* can mean *inappropriate,* that denotation does not fit the context.
> - **H** is incorrect because *inspired* does not contrast with *graceful, confident,* and *controlled*.

TEKS 1B

9 What tone or attitude toward the characters does the author's use of third-person omniscient point of view create?

A Lack of interest in any particular character

B Sympathy for the experiences of both the boy and the girl

C Exasperation at the problems of teenagers

D Amusement at the emotions of all the characters

> **EXPLANATION:** In third-person omniscient point of view, the narrator is able to reveal the thoughts and feelings of all the characters. **B** is correct. The narrator presents the experiences of the boy and the girl in a straightforward way that allows readers to feel sympathy for both of them.
> - **A** is incorrect because the narrator seems interested in the characters' experiences.
> - **C** and **D** are incorrect because the narrator presents the characters' experiences and emotions in an evenhanded way, expressing neither exasperation nor amusement.

TEKS 5C

GO ON ➡

Use "How to Become a Writer" and "For the Love of the Dance" (pp. 47–51) to answer questions 10–12.

10 In what way are the boy who writes to Keller and the boy in the story similar?

F   Both have an ambition.
G   Both are extremely creative.
H   Both are tall and thin.
J   Both are blind.

> **EXPLANATION:** The boy who writes to Keller wants to become an author. The boy in the story wants to create dances. **F** is correct.
> • **G** is incorrect. While the boy in the story is creative, the reader knows nothing about how creative the boy who writes to Keller is.
> • **H** is incorrect. No details in the letter describe the boy's physical appearance.
> • **J** is incorrect. The boy who writes to Keller is blind, but the boy in the story is not.

Fig. 19A, 19B

11 Both selections explore themes and ideas about —

A   personal handicaps
B   creativity
C   writing
D   dancing

> **EXPLANATION:** The letter addresses the creative process of writing, and the story deals with the creative process of dancing. **B** is correct.
> • **A** is incorrect. Only the letter deals with personal handicaps, and it is not the primary focus.
> • **C** is incorrect. Only the letter deals with writing.
> • **D** is incorrect. Only the story deals with dancing.

TEKS 2A; Fig. 19B

12 One literary technique that both the letter and the story use is —

F   foreshadowing
G   omniscient narrator
H   metaphor
J   dialogue

> **EXPLANATION: H** is correct. A metaphor is an imaginative comparison between two things that are basically unlike each other. For example, Keller compares a writer to a pioneer blazing a new trail, while the narrator of the story compares the boy to an ugly duckling who becomes a graceful swan.
> • **F** is incorrect. Only the story uses foreshadowing.
> • **G** is incorrect. Only the story has an omniscient narrator.
> • **J** is incorrect. Only the story uses dialogue.

TEKS 6; Fig. 19A

GO ON

Answer the following question in the space provided.

13 What message do the authors of "How to Become a Writer" and "For the Love of the Dance" share? Support your answer with evidence from **both** selections.

EXPLANATION

Rubric, high-scoring response:

- Reflects a perceptive awareness of text meaning and complexities; makes meaningful connections across the texts
- Uses specific, well-chosen evidence from the texts, supporting validity of response
- Shows deep understanding of the texts through ideas and supporting text evidence

Sample Response: Both authors communicate the message that originality is the key to creativity. Keller states this theme directly: "in order to be authors ourselves . . . we must strike into a path where no one has preceded us." Earlier in her letter, she points out that studying the best models of style and reading autobiographies of great writers are helpful, but that ultimately the talented writer knows how to write well by the time he or she has something original to say. The message in the story is similar. The boy is able to dance well only when he is presenting a dance that he has choreographed himself. The last sentence of the story underscores the importance of finding a creative path no one else has traveled: the boy remains awkward "except when . . . dancing to the beat of his own drummer."

TEKS 2A; Fig. 19A, 19B

STOP

Reading Practice

Reading Practice

Read this selection. Then answer the questions that follow.

Water Names

by Lan Samantha Chang

My notes about
what I am reading

1   Summertime at dusk we'd gather on the back porch,
tired and sticky from another day of fierce encoded quarrels,
nursing our mosquito bites and frail dignities, sisters in name
only. At first we'd pinch and slap each other, fighting for the
best—least ragged—folding chair. Then we'd argue over
who would sit next to our grandmother. We were so close
together on the tiny porch that we often pulled our own hair
by mistake. Forbidden to bite, we planted silent toothmarks
on each other's wrists. We ignored the bulk of house behind
us, the yard, the fields, the darkening sky. We even forgot
about our grandmother. Then suddenly we'd hear her old, dry
voice, very close, almost on the backs of our necks.

2   "*Xiushila!* Shame on you. Fighting like a bunch of
chickens."

3   And Ingrid, the oldest, would freeze with her thumb and
forefinger right on the back of Lily's arm. I would slide my
hand away from the end of Ingrid's braid. Ashamed, we
would shuffle our feet while Waipuo calmly found her chair.

4   On some nights she sat with us in silence, the tip of her
cigarette glowing red like a distant stoplight. But on some
nights she told us stories, "just to keep up your Chinese," she
said, and the red dot flickered and danced, making ghostly
shapes as she moved her hands like a magician in the dark.

5   "In these prairie crickets I often hear the sound of rippling
waters, of the Yangtze River," she said. "Granddaughters,
you are descended on both sides from people of the water
country, near the mouth of the great Chang Jiang, as it is
called, where the river is so grand and broad that even on
clear days you can scarcely see the other side.

"Water Names" from *Hunger: A Novella and Stories* by Lan Samantha Chang.
Copyright © 1998 by Lan Samantha Chang. Reprinted by permission of W.W. Norton &
Company, Inc. and The Wylie Agency.

Name _____ Date _____

My notes about
what I am reading

6　"The Chang Jiang runs four thousand miles, originating in the Himalaya mountains where it crashes, flecked with gold dust, down steep cliffs so perilous and remote that few humans have ever seen them. In central China, the river squeezes through deep gorges, then widens in its last thousand miles to the sea. Our ancestors have lived near the mouth of this river, the ever-changing delta, near a city called Nanjing, for more than a thousand years."

7　"A thousand years," murmured Lily, who was only ten. When she was younger she had sometimes burst into nervous crying at the thought of so many years. Her small insistent fingers grabbed my fingers in the dark.

8　"Through your mother and I you are descended from a line of great men and women. We have survived countless floods and seasons of ill-fortune because we have the spirit of the river in us. Unlike mountains, we cannot be powdered down or broken apart. Instead, we run together, like raindrops. Our strength and spirit wear down mountains into sand. But even our people must respect the water."

9　She paused, and a bit of ash glowed briefly as it drifted to the floor.

10　"When I was young, my own grandmother once told me the story of Wen Zhiqing's daughter. Twelve hundred years ago the civilized parts of China still lay to the north, and the Yangtze valley lay unspoiled. In those days lived an ancestor named Wen Zhiqing, a resourceful man, and proud. He had been fishing for many years with trained cormorants, which you girls of course have never seen. Cormorants are sleek, black birds with long, bending necks which the fishermen fitted with metal rings so the fish they caught could not be swallowed. The birds would perch on the side of the old wooden boat and dive into the river." We had only known blue swimming pools, but we tried to imagine the sudden shock of cold and the plunge, deep into water.

11　"Now, Wen Zhiqing had a favorite daughter who was very beautiful and loved the river. She would beg to go out on the boat with him. This daughter was a restless one, never contented with their catch, and often she insisted they stay

Reading Practice
© Houghton Mifflin Harcourt Publishing Company

out until it was almost dark. Even then, she was not satisfied. She had been spoiled by her father, kept protected from the river, so she could not see its danger. To this young woman, the river was as familiar as the sky. It was a bright, broad road stretching out to curious lands. She did not fully understand the river's depths.

My notes about what I am reading

12 "One clear spring evening, as she watched the last bird dive off into the blackening waters, she said, 'If only this catch would bring back something more than another fish!'

13 "She leaned over the side of the boat and looked at the water. The stars and moon reflected back at her. And it is said that the spirits living underneath the water looked up at her as well. And the spirit of a young man who had drowned in the river many years before saw her lovely face."

14 We had heard about the ghosts of the drowned, who wait forever in the water for a living person to pull down instead. A faint breeze moved through the mosquito screens and we shivered.

15 "The cormorant was gone for a very long time," Waipuo said, "so long that the fisherman grew puzzled. Then, suddenly, the bird emerged from the waters, almost invisible in the night. Wen Zhiqing grasped his catch, a very large fish, and guided the boat back to shore. And when Wen reached home, he gutted the fish and discovered, in its stomach, a valuable pearl ring."

16 "From the man?" said Lily.

17 "Sshh, she'll tell you."

18 Waipuo ignored us. "His daughter was delighted that her wish had been fulfilled. What most excited her was the idea of an entire world like this, a world where such a beautiful ring would be only a bauble! For part of her had always longed to see faraway things and places. The river had put a spell on her heart. In the evenings she began to sit on the bank, looking at her own reflection in the water. Sometimes she said she saw a handsome young man looking back at her. And her yearning for him filled her heart with sorrow and fear, for she knew that she would soon leave her beloved family.

19   "'It's just the moon,' said Wen Zhiqing, but his daughter shook her head. 'There's a kingdom under the water,' she said. 'The prince is asking me to marry him. He sent the ring as an offering to you.' 'Nonsense,' said her father, and he forbade her to sit by the water again.

20   "For a year things went as usual, but the next spring there came a terrible flood that swept away almost everything. In the middle of a torrential rain, the family noticed that the daughter was missing. She had taken advantage of the confusion to hurry to the river and visit her beloved. The family searched for days but they never found her."

21   Her smoky, rattling voice came to a stop.

22   "What happened to her?" Lily said.

23   "It's okay, stupid," I told her. "She was so beautiful that she went to join the kingdom of her beloved. Right?"

24   "Who knows?" Waipuo said. "They say she was seduced by a water ghost. Or perhaps she lost her mind to desiring."

25   "What do you mean?" asked Ingrid.

26   "I'm going inside," Waipuo said, and got out of her chair with a creak. A moment later the light went on in her bedroom window. We knew she stood before the mirror, combing out her long, wavy silver-gray hair, and we imagined that in her youth she too had been beautiful.

27   We sat together without talking, breathing our dreams in the lingering smoke. We had gotten used to Waipuo's abruptness, her habit of creating a question and leaving without answering it, as if she were disappointed in the question itself. We tried to imagine Wen Zhiqing's daughter. What did she look like? How old was she? Why hadn't anyone remembered her name?

28   While we weren't watching, the stars had emerged. Their brilliant pinpoints mapped the heavens. They glittered over us, over Waipuo in her room, the house, and the small city we lived in, the great waves of grass that ran for miles around us, the ground beneath as dry and hard as bone.

GO ON

Use "Water Names" (pp. 60–63) to answer questions 1–9.

1 What is the most likely reason Waipuo told her granddaughters the story about Wen Zhiqing's daughter?

  A She wants them to feel a connection with their Chinese heritage and family tradition.

  B She wants to warn them against playing around a dangerous pond or river.

  C She wants them to understand what life was like when she was their age.

  D She hopes they will find husbands as handsome as the prince from the river.

2 Which line from the selection best shows the relationship between past and present?

  F *At first we'd pinch and slap each other, fighting for the best—least ragged—folding chair.*

  G *Cormorants are sleek, black birds with long, bending necks which the fishermen fitted with metal rings so the fish they caught could not be swallowed.*

  H *"In these prairie crickets I often hear the sound of rippling waters, of the Yangtze River," she said.*

  J *She had taken advantage of the confusion to hurry to the river and visit her beloved.*

3 Which of the following are the best synonyms for the words "perilous and remote" in paragraph 6?

  A Haunting and beautiful

  B Dangerous and isolated

  C Exciting and distant

  D High and fast-moving

4 Which statement best describes the plot structure of this story?

  F A grandmother tells how one of her granddaughters died in a flood.

  G A young girl tells about seeing a young man beneath the water of a river.

  H A grandmother tells about an incident from her childhood.

  J A grandmother tells an old story to her grandchildren.

5 What most likely happened to Wen Zhiqing's daughter?

  A She married the underwater prince.

  B She ran away to America.

  C She drowned in the flood.

  D She was killed trying to save her father.

6 A symbol in the story that represents the family's Chinese heritage is —

  F the river water

  G the night

  H the stars

  J the glowing cigarette

GO ON

7 Which passage from the story suggests that the grandmother comes from an oral storytelling tradition?

   A *Shame on you. Fighting like a bunch of chickens.*

   B *. . . the red dot flickered and danced, making ghostly shapes as she moved her hands like a magician in the dark.*

   C *She paused, and a bit of ash glowed briefly as it drifted to the floor.*

   D *"I'm going inside," Waipuo said. . . . A moment later the light went on in her bedroom window.*

8 At the end of the story, what does "the ground beneath as dry and hard as bone" symbolize?

   F The narrator's realization that her grandmother will soon die

   G The bleakness of the family's life in the United States

   H Waipuo's dry sense of humor

   J The family's physical separation from their heritage

9 Which statement best conveys a major theme of the story?

   A Disobeying parents will often lead to bad consequences.

   B It is better to live in a prairie region than in one that is threatened by floods.

   C Deep longings can be dangerous if a person gets carried away by them.

   D Fishing can be a dangerous way of life.

Answer the following question in the space provided.

10 Compare and contrast the modern characters in "Water Names" with those in the traditional tale told by Waipuo. What role does Waipuo play in the story? Support your answer with evidence from the story.

Reading Practice

Read this selection. Then answer the questions that follow.

Paper Airplanes

by Kyoko Mori

My notes about
what I am reading

Kyoko Mori was born in Japan but moved to the United States as a teenager to attend college. She now teaches creative writing in addition to publishing her own work.

1   What I miss most from not having a family close by is a sense that the past is an open and growing manuscript, expansive and forgiving. When we talk about the past with family, we often find that each of us remembers different aspects of the same experience. Though the difference in memory can sometimes lead to bickering, it's a relief to know that none of us has the sole responsibility for remembering— what we forget will be recalled by someone else. We occasionally learn details we didn't know because we were too young at the time or lived too far away. Family stories can shed a new light on the events we think we know. After the conversation, we add the new pieces to our memory. In this way, the past can expand rather than shrink. I look forward to seeing my mother's family on my short visits to Japan because that's one of the few times I can experience memory expanding.

2   The last time I saw my uncle, Kenichi, he had just finished reading my first novel, *Shizuko's Daughter,* in the Japanese translation. Many of the details in the novel's setting come from my grandparents' house in the country—the house where Kenichi had grown up. He was glad that I had included the child's wooden slide my grandfather built when my mother was born, the purple lantern flowers my grandmother used to grow, the cicadas that were always buzzing in the trees in the yard.

3   "I was amazed by how much you could remember," he said.

Excerpt from *Polite Lies: On Being a Woman Caught Between Cultures* by Kyoko Mori. Text copyright © 1997 by Kyoko Mori. Reprinted by permission of Henry Holt and Company, LLC.

4   "Of course I remember a lot," I reassured him. His own kids, fifteen years younger than I, do not recall our grandparents in the same way—they were just babies when our grandfather died; by the time they were growing up, our grandmother was in her eighties and no longer able to take long walks with them or grow as many flowers in her garden as she used to. Kenichi was happy to have me remember and write about what his kids could not, so that the memories are kept alive.

5   "There's one thing I felt really bad about," Kenichi confessed. "I thought about it the whole time I was reading your novel."

6   "What was that?" I asked him, leaning forward over the table where we were having dinner.

7   "Remember those diaries your mother kept when she was in high school?" he asked. "There were many of them, in those glossy, yellow notebooks."

8   "Yes," I said. "I have them." Shortly after I left for college, my grandmother had found them in the attic of her house and sent them to me.

9   "But you don't have all the volumes," Kenichi said. "Do you know why?"

10   I shook my head. There were a few months missing here and there, but I always assumed that one or two notebooks must have gotten misplaced.

11   "When your mother finished high school and was in Kobe, working as a secretary, I was living in that house in the country with your grandparents and your Aunt Keiko. We were just kids." Kenichi paused.

12   I nodded, encouraging him to go on. Kenichi is sixteen years younger than my mother, who was the oldest of six children.

13   "Those diaries were already in the attic then. When I was in grade school, I found them there. The notebooks had such beautiful white paper—thick and glossy. I was only eight or nine, you have to remember. I tore the pages out and made paper airplanes. Every day, I would sit on top of the stairs, tear out page after page of your mother's diary, and fold paper airplanes. I watched them flying down the stairs. I got pretty good at folding planes. Some of them went quite a long way. That's how a couple of those notebooks got lost. When I read your novel, I remembered that and felt so bad." Kenichi made a face. "I can't believe how stupid I was as a kid," he concluded.

My notes about what I am reading

14   "Don't worry about it," I said, feeling suddenly so happy that I was laughing. I was imagining hundreds of white paper airplanes flying. "Your telling me about it now makes up for everything."

15   I'm not sure if Kenichi was convinced. I couldn't explain my feelings to him very well. But maybe it doesn't matter. In the book of my past, there is now an image of my uncle as a boy sitting on a stairway and flying paper airplanes, made of beautiful paper, with my mother's words in their precise creases. Kenichi might think that each plane deprived me of a page of my mother's writing, a page of memory, but the opposite is true. I see those planes floating down the stairway toward me, passed on from Kenichi to me because we share a past and we both loved my mother—because we belong to the same family. I cannot ask for more, except the impossible: that I had the eloquence to tell my uncle, in his language, what I can only write in mine.

Name _____ Date _____

1 Which of the following best describes the author's purpose for writing "Paper Airplanes"?

A To provide a profile of her uncle, Kenichi, in Japan

B To point out that family members never agree about what they remember

C To show how family stories can expand our memory of the past

D To express her longing to return to the land of her childhood

2 What effect does the writer's use of dialogue have on the reader?

F It draws the reader closer to both the author and her uncle.

G It makes the reader feel immersed in the culture of Japan.

H It illustrates that family members often argue about memories.

J It shows the personality of her uncle while allowing her to remain detached.

3 Which sentence from the selection includes a sensory detail that creates a vivid image in the reader's mind?

A *I was only eight or nine, you have to remember.*

B *The notebooks had such beautiful white paper—thick and glossy.*

C *Remember those diaries your mother kept when she was in high school?*

D *Many of the details in the novel's setting come from my grandparents' house in the country—the house where Kenichi had grown up.*

4 In the last paragraph of the selection, what feelings does the author experience when she reflects on her uncle's story?

F Patience and forgiveness

G Amusement and relief

H Surprise and disappointment

J Delight and gratitude

5 Kenichi's story of the paper airplanes makes the author feel happy because —

A she knows how much her uncle loved airplanes when he was a boy

B she has a new memory to add to the book of her past

C her uncle is pleased with her novel

D she looks forward to writing about it someday

6 What is the purpose of paragraph 2?

F To introduce the topic of family stories

G To summarize the author's first novel

H To connect the novel's descriptions with her uncle's memories

J To present a revealing dialogue between herself and her uncle

7 Part of the author's diction is the use of metaphors. Which of the following is an example of this literary device?

A *I see those planes floating down the stairway. . . .*

B *[T]he past is an open and growing manuscript. . . .*

C *I tore the pages out and made paper airplanes.*

D *There were a few months missing here and there. . . .*

GO ON

Answer the following question in the space provided.

8 What is the controlling idea in "Paper Airplanes"? Support your answer with evidence from the selection.

Reading Practice
© Houghton Mifflin Harcourt Publishing Company

STOP

Name _____   Date _____

Reading Practice

Read this selection. Then answer the questions that follow.

The Runaway

by Robert Frost

My notes about
what I am reading

Once when the snow of the year was beginning to fall,
We stopped by a mountain pasture to say, "Whose colt?"
A little Morgan had one forefoot on the wall,
The other curled at his breast. He dipped his head
5   And snorted at us. And then he had to bolt.
We heard the miniature thunder where he fled,
And we saw him, or thought we saw him, dim and gray,
Like a shadow against the curtain of falling flakes.
"I think the little fellow's afraid of the snow.
10 He isn't winter-broken. It isn't play
With the little fellow at all. He's running away.
I doubt if even his mother could tell him, 'Sakes,[1]
It's only weather.' He'd think she didn't know!
Where is his mother? He can't be out alone."
15 And now he comes again with clatter of stone,
And mounts the wall again with whited eyes
And all his tail that isn't hair up straight.
He shudders his coat as if to throw off flies.
"Whoever it is that leaves him out so late,
20 When other creatures have gone to stall and bin,
Ought to be told to come and take him in."

1. **Sakes:** a shortened form of *for goodness' sake* or *for heaven's sake*, an expression of mild surprise or annoyance.

"The Runaway" from *The Poetry of Robert Frost*, edited by Edward Connery Lathem. Copyright © 1923, 1969 by Henry Holt and Company. Copyright © 1951 by Robert Frost. Reprinted by permission of Henry Holt and Company, LLC.

Use "The Runaway" (p. 72) to answer questions 1–4.

1 Which of the following best describes the speaker's thoughts and feelings about the colt?

   A The speaker is worried that the colt may be injured or frozen in the coming snowstorm.

   B Although the colt really has nothing to fear from the snow, the speaker pities him and feels the colt's owner should not have left him out.

   C The speaker wants to rescue the colt from the snowstorm but is afraid the colt will injure anyone who tries to catch him.

   D Although the colt is not in danger from the snowstorm, the speaker decides to take him back to his barn in order to teach the owner not to leave him out in the snow.

2 In line 6, the speaker refers to hearing the "miniature thunder" of the colt as he flees. What is the meaning of this phrase?

   F The colt is able to make a loud noise that frightens the listeners, even though it is snowing.

   G The colt represents the power of nature to do both good and harm to humans.

   H The colt, because it is small and weak, can produce only thunder and no lightning.

   J The colt is young and small, but it contains within itself the power of a full-grown horse.

3 Which of the following describes the rhyme scheme of the poem?

   A There is end rhyme, but it does not follow a regular pattern.

   B Every other line rhymes.

   C The poet does not use end rhyme.

   D The poem is divided into units of six lines with the repeating pattern *abacbc*.

4 In line 16, the speaker refers to the colt's "whited eyes." In what sense are the colt's eyes whited?

   F The colt's eyes are reflecting the snowfall in the meadow.

   G The blood has drained from the colt's eyes because of his fear of the coming snowstorm.

   H The colt's eyes are open so wide in fear that the white part of his eyes shows more than usual.

   J Snow has gotten into the frightened colt's eyes, making them look whiter than usual.

GO ON

Name _____ Date _____

Answer the following question in the space provided.

5 In "The Runaway," how does the poet's use of language inspire the reader's trust and confidence in the speaker's observations? Support your answer with evidence from the poem.

© Houghton Mifflin Harcourt Publishing Company

Reading Practice

Read this selection. Then answer the questions that follow.

from **Invasion from Mars**

by Howard Koch

My notes about
what I am reading

*This play is an excerpt from a radio drama that was first broadcast
in 1938. The plot is based on the novel* War of the Worlds *by H. G.
Wells. Koch's adaptation is presented as a series of news reports,
which led some of those first listeners to believe that the events
described were actually taking place.*

[*Fade in piano playing.*]

Announcer Two. Ladies and gentlemen, here is the latest
bulletin from the Intercontinental Radio News. Montreal,
Canada: Professor Morse of McGill University reports
5   observing a total of three explosions on the planet Mars
between the hours of 7:45 P.M. and 9:20 P.M. Eastern
Standard Time. This confirms earlier reports received from
American observatories. Now, nearer home, comes a special
announcement from Trenton, New Jersey. It is reported that
10   at 8:50 P.M. a huge, flaming object, believed to be a
meteorite,[1] fell on a farm in the neighborhood of Grovers Mill,
New Jersey, twenty-two miles from Trenton. The flash in the
sky was visible within a radius of several hundred miles and
the noise of the impact was heard as far north as Elizabeth.

15   We have dispatched a special mobile unit to the scene,
and will have our commentator, Mr. Phillips, give you a word
description as soon as he can reach there from Princeton. In
the meantime, we take you to the Hotel Martinet in Brooklyn,
where Bobby Millette and his orchestra are offering a
20   program of dance music.

[*Swing band for twenty seconds . . . then cut.*]

Announcer Two. We take you now to Grovers Mill,
New Jersey.

[*Crowd noises . . . police sirens.*]

---

1. **meteorite:** a stony or metallic mass that falls to Earth from space.

Excerpt from "Invasion from Mars" from *The Panic Broadcast* by Howard Koch.
Copyright © 1970 by Howard Koch. Reprinted by permission of International Creative
Management.

My notes about
what I am reading

25 **Phillips.** Ladies and gentlemen, this is Carl Phillips again, at
the Wilmuth farm, Grovers Mill, New Jersey. Professor
Pierson and myself made the eleven miles from Princeton in
ten minutes. Well, I . . . I hardly know where to begin, to paint
for you a word picture of the strange scene before my eyes,
30 like something out of a modern *Arabian Nights.*[2] Well, I just
got here. I haven't had a chance to look around yet. I guess
that's it. Yes, I guess that's the . . . thing, directly in front of
me, half buried in a vast pit. Must have struck with terrific
force. The ground is covered with splinters of a tree it must
35 have struck on its way down. What I can see of the . . . object
itself doesn't look very much like a meteor, at least not the
meteors I've seen. It looks more like a huge <u>cylinder</u>. It has a
diameter[3] of . . . what would you say, Professor Pierson?

Pierson [*off*]. About thirty yards.

40 **Phillips.** About thirty yards . . . The metal on the sheath
is . . . well, I've never seen anything like it. The color is sort of
yellowish-white. Curious spectators now are pressing close to
the object in spite of the efforts of the police to keep them
back. They're getting in front of my line of vision. Would you
45 mind standing on one side, please?

Policeman. One side, there, one side.

Phillips. While the policemen are pushing the crowd back,
here's Mr. Wilmuth, owner of the farm here. He may have
some interesting facts to add . . . Mr. Wilmuth, would you
50 please tell the radio audience as much as you remember of
this rather unusual visitor that dropped in your backyard?
Step closer, please. Ladies and gentlemen, this is Mr.
Wilmuth.

Wilmuth. I was listenin' to the radio.

55 **Phillips.** Closer and louder, please.

Wilmuth. Pardon me!

Phillips. Louder, please, and closer.

2. ***Arabian Nights:*** a reference to a large collection of stories and folk tales from the
Middle East and South Asia.
3. **diameter:** measurement of the width or thickness of an object, especially
a round or circular one.

My notes about
what I am reading

Wilmuth. Yes, sir—while I was listening to the radio and kinda drowsin', that professor fellow was talkin' about Mars,
60 so I was half dozin' and half . . .

Phillips. Yes, Mr. Wilmuth. Then what happened?

Wilmuth. As I was sayin', I was listenin' to the radio kinda halfways . . .

Phillips. Yes, Mr. Wilmuth, and then you saw something?

65 **Wilmuth.** Not first off. I heard something.

Phillips. And what did you hear?

Wilmuth. A hissing sound. Like this: sssssss . . . kinda like a fourt' of July rocket.

Phillips. Then what?

70 **Wilmuth.** Turned my head out the window and would have swore I was to sleep and dreamin'.

Phillips. Yes?

Wilmuth. I seen a kinda greenish streak and then zingo! Somethin' smacked the ground. Knocked me clear out of
75 my chair!

Phillips. Well, were you frightened, Mr. Wilmuth?

Wilmuth. Well, I—I ain't quite sure. I reckon I—I was kinda riled.

Phillips. Thank you, Mr. Wilmuth. Thank you.

80 **Wilmuth.** Want me to tell you some more?

Phillips. No . . . That's quite all right, that's plenty.

Ladies and gentlemen, you've just heard Mr. Wilmuth, owner of the farm where this thing has fallen. I wish I could convey the atmosphere . . . the background of this . . .
85 fantastic scene. Hundreds of cars are parked in a field in back of us. Police are trying to rope off the roadway leading into the farm. But it's no use. They're breaking right through.

Their headlights throw an enormous spot on the pit where the object's half buried. Some of the more daring souls are
90 venturing near the edge. Their silhouettes stand out against the metal sheen.

[*Faint humming sound.*]

One man wants to touch the thing . . . he's having an argument with a policeman. The policeman wins . . . Now,
95 ladies and gentlemen, there's something I haven't mentioned in all this excitement, but it's becoming more distinct. Perhaps you've caught it already on your radio. Listen: *(Long pause)* . . . Do you hear it? It's a curious humming sound that seems to come from inside the object. I'll move
100 the microphone nearer. Here. *(Pause)* Now we're not more than twenty-five feet away. Can you hear it now? Oh, Professor Pierson!

Pierson. Yes, Mr. Phillips?

Phillips. Can you tell us the meaning of that scraping noise
105 inside the thing?

Pierson. Possibly the unequal cooling of its surface.

Phillips. Do you still think it's a meteor, Professor?

Pierson. I don't know what to think. The metal casing is definitely extraterrestrial . . . not found on this earth.
110 Friction with the earth's atmosphere usually tears holes in a meteorite. This thing is smooth and, as you can see, of cylindrical shape.

Phillips. Just a minute! Something's happening! Ladies and gentlemen, this is terrific! This end of the thing is beginning to
115 flake off! The top is beginning to rotate like a screw! The thing must be hollow!

Voices. She's a movin'!

Look, the darn thing's unscrewing!

My notes about
what I am reading

My notes about
what I am reading

Keep back, there! Keep back, I tell you!

120   Maybe there's men in it trying to escape!

It's red hot, they'll burn to a cinder!

Keep back there. Keep those idiots back!

[*Suddenly the clanking sound of a huge piece of falling metal.*]

125   **Voices.** She's off! The top's loose!

Look out there! Stand back!

Phillips. Ladies and gentlemen, this is the most terrifying thing I have ever witnessed . . . Wait a minute! *Someone's crawling out of the hollow top.* Someone or . . . something.
130   I can see peering out of that black hole two luminous disks . . . Are they eyes? It might be a face. It might be . . .

[*Shout of awe from the crowd.*]

Phillips. Good heavens, something's wriggling out of the shadow like a gray snake. Now it's another one, and another.
135   They look like tentacles to me. There, I can see the thing's body. It's large as a bear and it glistens like wet leather. But that face. It . . . it's indescribable. I can hardly force myself to keep looking at it. The eyes are black and gleam like a serpent. The mouth is V-shaped with saliva dripping from its
140   rimless lips that seem to quiver and pulsate. The monster or whatever it is can hardly move. It seems weighed down by . . . possibly gravity or something. The thing's rising up. The crowd falls back. They've seen enough. This is the most extraordinary experience. I can't find words . . . I'm pulling
145   this microphone with me as I talk. I'll have to stop the description until I've taken a new position. Hold on, will you please, I'll be back in a minute.

[*Fade into piano.*]

Use the excerpt from "Invasion from Mars" (pp. 75–79) to answer questions 1–7.

1 The word <u>cylinder</u> in line 37 comes from the Greek word *kulindein,* which means "to roll." A cylinder is —

A a flat, level surface

B smooth and log-shaped

C a long rectangular shape

D a pyramid

2 What is the main purpose of lines 117–126?

F To increase the mood of suspense

G To add details that build understanding of the alien

H To provide a "scientific" explanation of the mysterious object

J To reveal the climax of the play

3 An archetype is a model or pattern that is repeated in literature across cultures and time. By using an archetypal image of the alien in lines 133–140, the playwright is —

A decreasing the tension of the turning point

B leading the action of the play in an unexpected direction

C providing new insights into life on other planets

D capitalizing on people's worst fears about extraterrestrial creatures

4 Which line from the play is an example of sensory language?

F *This is the most extraordinary experience.*

G *But that face. It . . . it's indescribable.*

H *The mouth is V-shaped with saliva dripping from its rimless lips. . . .*

J *. . . I've never seen anything like it.*

5 The playwright uses ellipses throughout the play to —

A show where text has been deleted from the original version

B indicate where the sound of static should make the words unintelligible

C reflect the slowness with which events are unfolding

D emphasize the commentator's difficulty in comprehending what he is seeing

6 The commentator's tone, or attitude, by the end of the play can best be described as —

F objective

G panicky

H cautious

J eager

7 Which inference is most clearly supported by details at the end of the excerpt?

A The conflict is about to intensify.

B The conflict will rapidly be resolved.

C The suspense will decrease as the rest of the play unfolds.

D The setting will shift to outer space.

GO ON

Answer the following question in the space provided.

8 Why does the playwright include the scene in which the commentator interviews Mr. Wilmuth? Explain your answer and support it with evidence from the play.

Reading Practice

Read this selection. Then answer the questions that follow.

from Advertising on the Brain: How to Outsmart the Power of Advertising

by Margie Markarian

My notes about
what I am reading

1   When Aidan T., 13, saw the iPod touch commercial promising "good, good times around the bend," he knew it was the iPod for him. The ad's 30 seconds of high-energy music, eye-popping graphics, and in-your-face camera angles were all he needed to see.

2   "It looked awesome and had all these really cool applications," says Aidan, an eighth grader who lives in Franklin, Mass. A few months later, Aidan plunked down money he had been saving to become the first of his friends to own one of the slick gadgets. He's now the go-to guy for questions about the latest apps, games, and other downloads.

3   Aidan's positive reaction to the commercial is what iPod maker Apple and other companies have in mind when they create advertising. Most ads aren't designed for the part of your brain that controls reasoning, called the *prefrontal cortex.* Instead, they target the part of the brain that controls your emotions. The hub of that section is called the *amygdala.* Speaking to your emotions is a powerful way to grab your attention, make a lasting impression, and get you to spend money at the mall.

4   "Advertisers know how our brains are wired," explains Erin Walsh, coordinator of the MediaWise programs at the National Institute on Media and the Family. "They know the pathway to the emotional brain is faster than the pathway to your logical-thinking brain." That's why many ads don't tell you practical details about how a product is made or what it will cost at the store.

5   Once your emotions are aroused, it's easy to link them to a specific product. Advertisements often make that

---

Excerpt from "Advertising on the Brain: How to outsmart the power of advertising" by Margie Markarian from *Current Health* 1, Vol. 33, Issue 2, October 2009. Text copyright © 2009 by Weekly Reader Corporation. Reprinted by permission of Weekly Reader Corporation and Packaged Facts.

connection for you by dangling tempting promises. "'You'll be the coolest kid in school if you use a certain hair gel' or 'you'll be hosting fun parties with lots of friends if you own a particular video game'" are two examples, says Latoya Peterson. She is a spokesperson for the Center for a New American Dream, an organization that helps people be responsible consumers.

My notes about what I am reading

Advertising Overload

6   Advertising is everywhere. On average, American kids see about 40,000 TV commercials a year. When you start counting print ads, radio commercials, billboards, signs around town, Internet ads, and previews at the movies, that number soars much higher. You may not even be aware of all the different types of advertising you see throughout the day.

7   "Any product or box with a name on it is a form of advertising," says Douglas Gentile. He is a professor who runs the Media Research Lab at Iowa State University. "If you're wearing a shirt with a logo, it's advertising. So is a can of Coke and the box of cereal on your breakfast table in the morning."

8   When you see your favorite character on TV, in a movie, or in a video game using a specific brand-name product, it's most likely because a company paid for it to be there. That is called product placement, and it's one of the fastest-growing forms of advertising. The Transformers movies are filled with product placements for General Motors cars. In *Gossip Girl,* Blair and Serena text and chat using the trendiest Verizon phones.

9   Brand names are even showing up in songs and popular book series. When Sharpay sings about her pink Prada tote and Tiffany hair band in *High School Musical 2* she's hyping products. There's also subtle product promotion happening when characters in the Clique books strut around in Ralph Lauren skinny jeans or teen spy Alex Rider whips out a specially equipped Game Boy to escape danger in *Stormbreaker,* by Anthony Horowitz.

Ways to Be Smart About Advertising

10   Advertising is a part of life. It helps pay for the TV shows you watch, the Web sites you surf, the social networks you use, and the magazines you read. Becoming media smart is the best way to make sure you're not pressured into buying things you don't really need or want. These tips will help you become a smarter consumer:

GO ON

11   **Realize that advertising is always trying to sell you something.** As entertaining as some ads can be, remember that ads are a form of persuasive speech. "Don't treat them like a friend," advises Gentile. "Sit there with your arms crossed, and look at them skeptically. That will slow down their effect somewhat."

12   **Watch commercials more carefully.** Walsh suggests making a game of it by watching commercials with family or friends. "After the first 20 seconds, stop [the commercial] and list all the emotional tricks you see and hear," she says. Typical tricks include hip-looking kids in hot fashions, great music, fun camera angles, unusual lighting techniques, celebrities, and comical situations. "You might not even be able to figure out what the commercial is for because product names often don't get mentioned until the very end," Walsh says.

13   **Analyze marketing messages in all forms of advertising.** To do this, says Cynthia Scheibe, a developmental psychologist and media literacy expert with Project Look Sharp at Ithaca College in New York, ask yourself some critical-thinking questions. Those include:

- Who paid for the commercial or print ad? Why do they want to get your attention?
- Who is the target audience?
- What kinds of lifestyles or values are being represented? Are they glamorized? If so, in what ways?
- Is this ad sending a healthy or an unhealthy message? How so?
- What is the literal, or exact, meaning of the message's words and images?
- What are the hidden or suggested messages behind the ad's words and images?

14   The goal of being media smart isn't to bash advertising. "The goal is to teach people to think critically about the ads they see," Scheibe says. "Sometimes advertising is very informative, and there are some good products out there that you wouldn't know about without it."

GO ON

Teen Spending Power

If you're wondering why marketers are so eager to get your attention, follow the money trail. Twenty-six million people ages 12 to 17 control $80 billion of their own spending money. That same group also influences about $110 billion of family spending. Among all teens, the biggest categories of spending are clothes and entertainment. When it comes to girls versus boys, here's how the spending breaks down.

Top Five Things Teenagers Spend Money On	
GIRLS	**BOYS**
1. Clothing	1. Video games
2. Jewelry and accessories	2. Electronics
3. Makeup	3. Clothing
4. Music	4. Music
5. Movies	5. Movies

GO ON

Use the excerpt from "Advertising on the Brain" (pp. 82–85) to answer questions 1–5.

1 In paragraphs 3 and 4, what type of evidence does the author provide to support the claim that advertisements are designed to appeal to people's emotions?

A Statistics

B Anecdotes and examples

C Facts and expert views

D Logical reasons

2 Which of the following best states the controlling idea of the section titled "Advertising Overload"?

F Most advertising is "in-your-face" because advertisers want to have a big impact on consumers.

G Advertising is found in popular movies that appeal to young people.

H Teenagers are surrounded by advertising every day, although some of it is almost too subtle to notice.

J Advertisers who want to reach teenagers shouldn't waste their money on old-fashioned TV advertisements.

3 Which of the following is a valid conclusion to draw from the chart on page 85?

A Boys spend more money on clothing than girls do.

B Teenagers spend $80 billion dollars on clothing and video games each year.

C Girls and boys spend equal amounts of money on electronics.

D Boys and girls both spend much of their money on music and movies.

4 Which of the following best summarizes the section titled "Ways to Be Smart About Advertising"?

F It's not possible to avoid advertising, and sometimes ads provide good information. However, you should understand the purpose of advertising and carefully analyze the ads you see.

G In this section, the author provides some excellent tips for analyzing advertisements. Teenagers who apply these tips will be well on their way to becoming smarter consumers.

H Consumers need to know that advertising is not their friend. They should analyze each ad with a critical eye because most ads have an unhealthy message hidden behind the glamour.

J Analyzing TV commercials with your friends and family can be more fun than watching the actual television shows. Just be careful you are not persuaded to buy anything.

5 The author's overall purpose in this article is to —

A summarize advertising techniques that have the most effect on teens

B teach teenagers to become more critical consumers of advertising

C present an insider's view on how advertising works

D analyze common messages that advertising sends to consumers

GO ON

Answer the following question in the space provided.

6 In "Advertising on the Brain," is the author critical of advertising, positive about advertising, or neutral? Explain your answer and support it with evidence from the selection.

Reading Practice

Read this selection. Then answer the questions that follow.

Moon Shot Sparks Distant Memories of a Questing America

by Edward Achorn

My notes about
what I am reading

The writer of this editorial responds to President Obama's proposal in 2010 to cut back funding for the space program.

1   When I was nine years old, I got an amazing Christmas present: a plastic G.I. Joe space capsule, by Hasbro,[1] modeled on the Project Mercury capsule that carried John Glenn into orbit around the world.

2   One of the great things about it was that it came with a 45 rpm record. (For the Digital Generation, that's a 7-inch-wide round piece of plastic with a hole in the middle that you put on an ancient contraption called a "record player," which scraped a needle across its surface to produce sound.)

3   That was probably my first record (a thousand followed, many of them related to the Beatles) and I must have listened to it a hundred times, marveling over the sound of a countdown and rockets blasting, of an astronaut talking to the ground crew at Cape Kennedy,[2] and of a no-nonsense narrator, speaking in a clipped, consonant-popping <u>patter</u> about the boundless promise of American know-how.

4   Last week, to my amazement, I found that record posted on the Internet in digital form, and listened to it for the first time in decades.

5   "Welcome to manned space exploration!"

6   There it was again, the voice of the proud, confident America of my youth.

---

1. **Hasbro:** a multinational toymaker and board game manufacturer.
2. **Cape Kennedy:** the name by which Cape Canaveral, the launching area in Florida for U.S. manned space missions, was known from 1963 to 1973.

"Moon shot sparks distant memories of a questing America" by Edward Achorn from *The Providence Journal*, April 27, 2010. Copyright © 2010 The Providence Journal Company. Reprinted by permission of The Providence Journal.

My notes about
what I am reading

7   "Mercury's primary purpose was to launch an American astronaut into orbit around the Earth, and then return him safely. This feat was successfully accomplished on Feb. 20, 1962, when John Glenn Jr. in Mercury's Friendship VII, completed a three-orbit flight," the announcer boasts.

8   Americans accomplished things in those days. There were disasters along the way, but Americans kept trying until they succeeded.

9   The record's flip side featured the recorded radio transmission of an astronaut in space.

10   "Roger, zero G [gravity], and I feel fine. Capsule is turning around. Oh, that view is tremendous!"

11   Hasbro knew what it was doing. Half the kids in America wanted to be astronauts.

12   Three years after this toy hit the shelves, Neil Armstrong stepped onto the surface of the moon and planted the American flag.

13   Snobby commentators like Erik Sevareid found the whole exercise dubious, an expression of America's obnoxious desire to accomplish great things for the sake of doing so, regardless of cost or danger. "It is possible that the divine spark in man will consume him in flames, that the big brain will prove our ultimate flaw, like the dinosaur's big body, that the metal plaque Armstrong and [Buzz] Aldrin expect to place on the moon will become man's epitaph," he said in his dour CBS commentary on July 15, 1969, on the eve of the Apollo 11 launch.

14   But I suspect many more Americans thought that the moon landing was something to be proud of, as a spectacular expression of the resilience, creativity and courage ingrained in the character of people who get to live in a place where they can achieve great things.

15   When Europeans arrived on these shores, they lived mostly as they had for centuries, using such primitive tools as plows pulled by oxen. It is stunning to stop and think that, within 200 years of the founding of the United States, an American had set his boot print on the moon and returned safely. That 476,000-mile round trip said as much about us as it did about a rocky extraterrestrial sphere.

16   The first human moon visitor was in the news the other day. Neil Armstrong sharply criticized President Obama's proposals for a stripped-down space program, as NASA devotes greater resources to confirming global-warming fears.

My notes about
what I am reading

17   "The . . . decision to cancel the Constellation program, its Ares 1 and Ares V rockets, and the Orion spacecraft, is devastating," he wrote in a letter co-signed by Apollo astronauts James Lovell and Eugene Cernan.

18   They complained that Americans will only have access to low Earth orbit and the International Space Station now through the Russian Soyuz program, at a cost of more than $50 million a seat, and that Mr. Obama's decision throws away $10 billion spent on Constellation.

19   Mr. Armstrong's moon mate, Buzz Aldrin, on the other hand, said the new plan makes perfect sense. We already went to the moon, he noted, and it is wiser to drop manned exploration for a while, encourage the development of lower-cost access to space and new technologies, and farm out some of the program to private interests.

20   It's an interesting debate. Obviously, the space program no longer grabs the public's imagination as it once did, and the president's shift in priorities reflects that reality.

21   But I wonder if anyone has factored other, less easily counted costs. Do we lose something when kids stop dreaming of leaving Earth's orbit—when they no longer study science because they can no longer hope to be astronauts? Do we lose some of our belief in ourselves when we cease being the undisputed leaders in space?

22   We're supposed to be embarrassed of our history these days, but I suspect the questing spirit that took human beings to these shores, that led them to conquer the West and that brought them to the moon still resides in America. It may lie dormant for a while, though.

Use "Moon Shot Sparks Distant Memories of a Questing America" (pp. 88–90)
to answer questions 1–6.

1 Which of the following best expresses the purpose of Achorn's editorial?

   A To describe a favorite childhood toy

   B To present his view that the space program is important in the lives of Americans

   C To explain the facts in favor of and against cutbacks in the space program

   D To highlight some of the major accomplishments of U.S. astronauts

2 Read the following dictionary entry.

> **patter** \păt´ər\ *n.* **1.** a series of light, soft tapping sounds **2.** jargon used by a particular group **3.** rapid speech **4.** meaningless talk

What is the definition of <u>patter</u> as it is used in paragraph 3?

   F Definition 1

   G Definition 2

   H Definition 3

   J Definition 4

3 What type of evidence does the writer present in paragraphs 1–7 to support his view of the space program?

   A Facts

   B Statistics

   C Anecdotes

   D Expert opinions

4 Read these sentences from paragraph 13.

> *Snobby commentators like Erik Sevareid found the whole exercise dubious, an expression of America's obnoxious desire to accomplish great things for the sake of doing so, regardless of cost or danger. "It is possible that the divine spark in man will consume him in flames . . . ," he said in his dour CBS commentary. . . .*

In these lines the writer uses the rhetorical fallacy known as —

   F personal attack

   G appeal to fear

   H stereotyping

   J appeal to pity

5 With which statement would the writer most likely agree?

   A NASA should focus on programs that will more directly benefit the human population.

   B Americans' questing nature will lead to their eventual downfall.

   C The occurrence of several disasters has eroded the glory of the space program.

   D The space program has always brought out the best in Americans.

GO ON

6 Examine the chart below.

Neil Armstrong	Buzz Aldrin
View: _____

1. The U.S. will have to pay millions for seats on the International Space Station if its own program is discontinued.
2. The U.S. will waste $10 billion already spent on Constellation if the program is cut. | View: Space program cuts will refocus priorities and stimulate other areas.

1. We have gone to the moon, so it is time to cut back on manned exploration.
2. The U.S. needs to encourage the development of lower-cost access to space. |

Which statement belongs in the blank?

F A cutback in the space program will cost money, not save it.

G Stricter regulations are needed to curb the government's excessive spending.

H Cutting back funding for the space program will lead to huge savings.

J It is time for other countries to take the lead in the space.

GO ON

Answer the following question in the space provided.

7 How does the structure of the writer's argument affect the persuasiveness of the editorial? Explain your answer and support it with evidence from the text.

Reading Practice
© Houghton Mifflin Harcourt Publishing Company

STOP

Reading Practice

Read the next two selections. Then answer the questions that follow.

Abalone, Abalone, Abalone

by Toshio Mori

My notes about
what I am reading

An abalone shell is shaped like an ear. The inside is colorful and has the luster, or shine, of a pearl. Because of this quality, abalone is often used to make jewelry or other ornaments.

1   Before Mr. Abe went away I used to see him quite often at his nursery. He was a carnation grower just as I am one today. At noontime I used to go to his front porch and look at his collection of abalone shells.

2   They were lined up side by side against the side of his house on the front porch. I was curious as to why he bothered to collect them. It was a lot of bother polishing them. I had often seen him sit for hours on Sundays and noon hours polishing each one of the shells with the greatest of care. Of course I knew these abalone shells were pretty. When the sun strikes the insides of these shells it is something beautiful to behold. But I could not understand why he continued collecting them when the front porch was practically full.

3   He used to watch for me every noon hour. When I approached he would look out of his room and bellow, "Hello, young man!"

4   "Hello, Abe-*san*,"[1] I said. "I came to see the abalone shells."

5   Then he came out of the house and we sat on the front porch. But he did not tell me why he collected these shells. I think I have asked him dozens of times but each time he closed his mouth and refused to answer.

6   "Are you going to pass this collection of abalone shells on to your children?" I said.

---

1. **san:** in the Japanese culture, a title of respect or courtesy added to the name of the person being addressed.

"Abalone, Abalone, Abalone" from *The Chauvinist and Other Stories* by Toshio Mori. Copyright © 1979 by the Regents of the University of California. Reprinted by permission of The UCLA Asian American Studies Center Press.

My notes about
what I am reading

7   "No," he said. "I want my children to collect for themselves. I wouldn't give it to them."

8   "Why?" I said. "When you die?"

9   Mr. Abe shook his head. "No. Not even when I die," he said. "I couldn't give the children what I see in these shells. The children must go out for themselves and find their own shells."

10   "Why, I thought this collecting hobby of abalone shells was a simple affair," I said.

11   "It is simple. Very simple," he said. But he would not tell me further.

12   For several years I went steadily to his front porch and looked at the beautiful shells. His collection was getting larger and larger. Mr. Abe sat and talked to me and on each occasion his hands were busy polishing the shells.

13   "So you are still curious?" he said.

14   "Yes," I said.

15   One day while I was hauling the old soil from the benches and replacing it with new soil I found an abalone shell half buried in the dust between the benches. So I stopped working. I dropped my wheelbarrow and went to the faucet and washed the abalone shell with soap and water. I had a hard time taking the grime off the surface.

16   After forty minutes of cleaning and polishing the old shell it became interesting. I began polishing both the outside and the inside of the shell. I found after many minutes of polishing that I could not do very much with the exterior side. It had scabs of the sea which would not come off by scrubbing and the surface itself was rough and hard. And in the crevices the grime stuck so that even with a needle it did not become clean.

17   But on the other side, the inside of the shell, the more I polished the more luster I found. It had me going.[2] There were colors which I had not seen in the abalone shells before or anywhere else. The different hues, running berserk in all directions, coming together in harmony. I guess I could say they were not unlike a rainbow which men once symbolized. As soon as I thought of this I thought of Mr. Abe.

2. **It had me going:** an expression that means "it seized my attention."

GO ON ➤

18   I remember running to his place, looking for him. "Abe-
      san!" I said when I found him. "I know why you are collecting
      the abalone shells!"

19   He was watering the carnation plants in the greenhouse.
      He stopped watering and came over to where I stood. He
      looked me over closely for awhile and then his face beamed.

20   "All right," he said. "Do not say anything. Nothing, mind
      you. When you have found the reason why you must collect
      and preserve them, you do not have to say anything more."

21   "I want you to see it, Abe-*san,*" I said.

22   "All right. Tonight," he said. "Where did you find it?"

23   "In my old greenhouse, half buried in the dust," I said.

24   He chuckled. "That is pretty far from the ocean," he said,
      "but pretty close to you."

25   At each noon hour I carried my abalone shell and
      went over to Mr. Abe's front porch. While I waited for his
      appearance I kept myself busy polishing the inside of the
      shell with a rag.

26   One day I said, "Abe-*san,* now I have three shells."

27   "Good!" he said. "Keep it up!"

28   "I have to keep them all," I said. "They are very much alike
      and very much different."

29   "Well! Well!" he said and smiled.

30   That was the last I saw of Abe-*san.* Before the month was
      over he sold his nursery and went back to Japan. He brought
      his collection along and thereafter I had no one to talk to
      at the noon hour. This was before I discovered the fourth
      abalone shell, and I should like to see Abe-*san* someday and
      watch his eyes roll as he studies me whose face is now akin
      to the collectors of shells or otherwise.

My notes about
what I am reading

from **Why Collect Books?**

This selection is from a journal about book collecting.

1   The world of book lovers is broken into two opposing and irreconcilable groups. The first, and much the largest, is made up of those who see books as <u>consumables</u>. The second, less common, includes those who see books as beautiful objects.

2   We will discuss book consumers first, and then dismiss them, for they need not concern us further. For these people, a book is a medium that carries the author's content—and that is all. When they read, they use the copy of the book in any way they please. When they are finished, they set it aside or discard it. These are the people who dog-ear corners, write shopping lists on endpapers, make marginal notes in ink, underline the text. For them, books are disposable items, intended to be used and then thrown away. The physical book is nothing more to them than a reader's fast food wrapper. . . .

3   Those of you who are left are the fortunate ones, and not nearly as uncommon as you might think. Although we are in the minority as regards the general population, there are still a great many of us. You might not think of yourselves as collectors, but you carry the virus. It may be latent, but be warned, it is chronic. There is no cure. The good news is that this disease, book collecting, gives pleasure and adds dimension to your life.

4   Those of us in the second group add another dimension, an aesthetic one, to our appreciation of books. We see books as physical objects of beauty and romance. While many of us do not necessarily define ourselves as book collectors, we love the look and feel of our books. Even if some of us do not understand first edition collecting, we have a shelf of treasured books, or even a library full of them.

"Why Collect Books?" from *Firsts Magazine.* Reprinted by permission of Firsts Magazine, Inc.

GO ON ➡

5   We tend to take care of our books in the same way we care for the other valuable objects we own, like paintings or posters. We see our collections as extensions of our interests, perhaps as a record of our intellectual and artistic experiences. Something about having a book on the shelf gives pleasure; owning books enriches our lives.

My notes about
what I am reading

6   Since collectors value books as beautiful objects, the books' condition is important. A lovely copy is more appealing than one that has been used and abused. One of our favorite book collectors says that she can read any book from cover to cover without leaving any evidence of having done so. While there are not many of us who can do this, all collectors take care with their books. Beginners may write their names in their books, but they would never purposely deface them, any more than they would carve graffiti into a sculpture or draw a moustache on a face in a painting.

7   For a collector, a book's edition is likely to be even more important than its condition. A Hemingway may always be a Hemingway, but a first edition is a world apart from a cheap paperback reading copy. There may have been a million copies of *The Sun Also Rises* printed over the years in all editions, but there were only 5,090 copies in the first edition. Only a few exist, fewer still in their original dust wrappers. There will never be any more copies of the first edition.

8   The underlying reason to collect books lies in the duality of the experience. Not only do collectors take pleasure from the intellectual content of their books, but they also enjoy the process of assembling their collections. At its most fundamental level, book collecting is an extension of the hunting-and-gathering instinct that has fired mankind's progress from prehistory. The thrill involved in finding a beautiful first edition is palpable, even for those of us who have been involved in the chase for many years.

9   Only yesterday, we had a conversation with a veteran bookseller who came upon a gloriously fresh first edition copy in dust jacket of Zora Neale Hurston's novel, *Their Eyes Were Watching God* (1937). Even though he had no economic interest in it, seeing and evaluating the book gave him pleasure. Finding a beautiful copy of a treasured book is a rewarding experience. Owning one gives continuing delight.

GO ON ➔

My notes about
what I am reading

10   There are many secondary reasons to collect, including economic ones. Many first edition books appreciate in value over time. The laws of supply and demand dictate that. Since books are fragile, the number of available copies in the marketplace tends to diminish over the years. The chances are that a collector's first edition library will become an increasingly valuable asset. There is a marketplace for books, and even though it has changed radically over the course of the last decade, book collecting is an expanding field that is likely to remain so.

11   Why collect books? Collect them because they are beautiful. Collect them because they are valuable. Most important of all, collect them because you love them.

12   If you are a collector, congratulations—and relax, you are not alone.

Use "Abalone, Abalone, Abalone" (pp. 94–96) to answer questions 1–7.

1 Why does the author describe the extent to which the narrator is puzzled by Mr. Abe's collecting?

A To give insight into the narrator's culture

B To explain the narrator's relationship with Mr. Abe

C To establish the narrator as unreliable

D To make the narrator's later shift in understanding more significant

2 Throughout the story, the narrator's tone, or attitude, toward Mr. Abe and his collecting is —

F earnest

G impatient

H humorous

J distant

3 The narrator wants Mr. Abe to see the abalone shell he finds because —

A he thinks he could sell it for a high price

B he finally realizes that each is unique

C it is an unusual shape and size

D it may not be abalone

4 In paragraph 17, the narrator describes the hues of the shell as "running berserk." In this context, berserk has the connotation of —

F insanely

G violently

H wildly

J emotionally

5 What does Mr. Abe mean when he says in paragraph 9 that his children must "find their own shells"?

A They do not like abalone shells.

B They must discover their own passions.

C He does not have enough shells to distribute equally among them.

D He plans to leave his collection to a museum.

6 The narrator treasures the first abalone shell he finds because it gives him —

F a reminder of his friendship with Mr. Abe

G an interesting hobby

H a way to decorate his porch

J a new view of the world

7 Which statement from the story identifies the turning point?

A *Before the month was over he sold his nursery. . . .*

B *While I waited for his appearance I kept myself busy polishing the inside of the shell with a rag.*

C *"I know why you are collecting the abalone shells!"*

D *[T]hese abalone shells were pretty.*

GO ON

Use the excerpt from "Why Collect Books?" (pp. 97–99) to answer questions 8–11.

8 Which words from paragraph 2 best help readers understand the meaning of the word <u>consumables</u> in paragraph 1?

   F *disposable items*

   G *underline the text*

   H *a medium that carries the author's content*

   J *dog-ear corners*

9 In paragraph 8, the author says that book collectors are like early hunter-gatherers because they —

   A feel the excitement of expanding their collections

   B pursue their hobby in groups

   C must be ruthless in their pursuit of a book

   D are forced to collect books out of need

10 According to the author, a fundamental characteristic of book collectors is that they —

   F collect only first editions

   G take care of their books

   H see their books as investments

   J display their books but never read them

11 The author's sentence structure and choice of words create a voice that is —

   A colloquial

   B stilted

   C conversational

   D lacking confidence

GO ON

© Houghton Mifflin Harcourt Publishing Company

Use "Abalone, Abalone, Abalone" and "Why Collect Books?" (pp. 94–99) to answer questions 12–13.

12 Which statement is supported by both selections?

F   One person's junk is another person's treasure.

G   Collecting can easily become an obsession.

H   Maintaining a collection can be as satisfying as building one.

J   Those who have large collections are much happier than those who have just a few items.

13 Both selections convey the idea that true collectors —

A   are motivated by a desire for profit

B   seek only that which is in good condition

C   are in a small minority

D   see meaning in objects beyond their economic value

Answer the following question in the space provided.

14 What similarities do the abalone shells and books share that make them worthy collectors' items? Explain your answer and support it with evidence from **both** selections.

Written Composition

Written Composition: Persuasive Essay 1

READ

Read the quotation in the box below.

> "Art is the window to man's soul. Without it he would never be able to see beyond his immediate world; nor could the world see the man within."
>
> *Lady Bird Johnson*

THINK

Should electives in the arts, such as music, art, and theater, continue to be offered even as schools face severe budget constraints? Consider how dropping these courses from your own school's curriculum could affect you and your fellow students.

WRITE

Write an editorial for your school newspaper in which you argue for or against eliminating courses in the arts to save money.

As you write your composition, remember to —

☐ craft a thesis that states whether or not you think these kinds of courses should be eliminated

☐ organize your reasons and supporting evidence logically and effectively

☐ develop your argument with strong reasons supported by facts, examples, description, and other relevant details

☐ make sure your composition is no longer than one page

TEKS 13A, 13B, 13C, 13D, 16A, 16D, 16E, 17, 18, 19

ANALYZE THE PROMPT

The prompt asks you to write an editorial expressing your position on cutting courses in the arts to save money. You must state your opinion, present reasons, support your reasons with evidence, and explain the significance of your facts and ideas.

RESPOND TO THE PROMPT

- **Plan** by stating your opinion and listing reasons that support it. Select the strongest and most convincing reasons. Then identify facts, examples, and other details that back up each reason.
- **Draft** your response by stating your position, or thesis. Present your reasons from weakest to strongest or in another order that makes sense. Explain each reason using relevant details.
- **Revise** to use more precise wording, to vary the lengths and types of your sentences, to insert additional evidence, and to add transitions to clarify the relationships between ideas.
- **Edit** to correct any errors in spelling, grammar, punctuation, or capitalization that could distract readers from being persuaded by your argument.

Benchmark Composition: Persuasive Essay 1   Score Point 4

Say No to a School Without the Arts!

"Art is the window to man's soul. Without it he would never be able to see beyond his immediate world; nor could the world see the man within." When Lady Bird Johnson said these words, I am sure she never envisioned a world without art. Yet that is what cutting music, art, and theater classes could lead to. Although all of these programs are equally important, the largest majority of our students take some sort of music. Eliminating music-related classes from our curriculum could save money in the short term for the district but would be very costly to many students in the long run.

First, some students come to school only because of their music classes. Without this incentive, they could lapse into truancy. Or, they might lose their motivation for keeping up their grades to be eligible to perform. Music classes also allow students who struggle with academics to succeed. This success, in turn, bolsters their self-esteem.

For many students, their music experience in high school can be a stepping stone to a greater future. Recently, on music career day, several alumni returned to talk to us. They included music teachers, performers, and even composers. Every one of them said how helpful their high school courses were in preparing them for their professions. Additionally, close to ninety percent of our students who apply to college music programs get some sort of related financial aid.

On paper, these cuts may look logical, since music is not subject to state testing. But, it has been proven that music classes enhance academic ability. In a study of second grade children, those who used piano keyboard training in addition to math software scored higher on math tests than those who used only the software. The College Entrance Examination Board just reported that students with experience in music performance or appreciation scored 57 and 63 points higher, respectively, on the verbal SAT and 41 and 44 points higher on the math SAT than students with no arts participation. If these statistics aren't eye-opening, then what is!

Music enriches our lives, provides us with a creative outlet, and sharpens skills that can help us succeed beyond high school. To cut the arts goes beyond closing the window; rather it is like slamming the door on our souls.

DEVELOPMENT OF IDEAS
The first paragraph ends with a clear statement of the writer's position, or thesis—that arts electives should not be removed from the curriculum. The thesis statement leads directly into the discussion of the reasons that support it.

ORGANIZATION/ PROGRESSION
The writer uses transitions, such as *first*, *or*, and *also* to help readers follow the progression of ideas and understand their relationship to each other.

ORGANIZATION/ PROGRESSION
The writer organizes supporting reasons in order of importance. The second reason, in paragraph 3, argues that music can affect a student's future success. The writer includes a statistic to support this point.

DEVELOPMENT OF IDEAS
In the fourth paragraph, the writer addresses an opposing view and then presents a counterargument, using supporting evidence that appeals to readers' logic.

Name _____ Date _____

This editorial skillfully argues against cuts in a school's music program, offering evidence that appeals to logic and emotions. The strongest reason is discussed last and counters an objection that readers might have with persuasive statistics and other facts. The conclusion summarizes the reasons and refers back to the opening quotation. The writing contains no distracting errors.

	ORGANIZATION/ PROGRESSION	DEVELOPMENT OF IDEAS	USE OF LANGUAGE CONVENTIONS
4	• Uses an effective organization for a persuasive essay that is skillfully structured to suit the purpose, audience, and context • Conveys ideas in a sustained, persuasive way • Uses clear transitions between ideas, sentences, and paragraphs	• Advances a clear thesis or position fully supported by logical reasons and reliable, relevant evidence, including facts, expert opinions, and/or quotations • Presents a full range of relevant perspectives • Uses effective rhetorical devices and appeals to logic, emotions, and ethical beliefs	• Shows strong understanding of appropriate word choice for the form, purpose, and tone of a persuasive essay • Uses purposeful, varied, and controlled sentences • Demonstrates consistent command of conventions so that writing is fluent and clear
3	• Uses a reasonably effective organization for a persuasive essay, with a structure appropriate to the purpose, audience, and context • Conveys ideas in a fairly sustained, persuasive way • Uses transitions between ideas, sentences, and paragraphs	• Advances a fairly clear thesis or position supported by logical reasons and reliable, relevant evidence • Presents a range of relevant perspectives • Uses rhetorical devices and appeals to logic, emotions, and ethical beliefs	• Shows basic understanding of word choice appropriate for a persuasive essay • Uses sentences that are purposeful, varied, and controlled for the most part • Demonstrates a good command of conventions; writing is mostly fluent and clear
2	• Uses a somewhat effective organization for a persuasive essay that shows some attention to purpose, audience, and context • Does not convey all ideas in a sustained, persuasive way • Uses too few transitions between ideas, sentences, and paragraphs	• Has an unclear thesis or position statement; thesis is supported by insufficient reasons and evidence • Presents few relevant perspectives other than the author's • Uses few rhetorical devices or appeals to logic, emotions, and ethical beliefs	• Shows some understanding of word choice; may be inappropriate to form, purpose, or tone • May use awkward, rambling sentences or unvaried sentence structure • Demonstrates limited command of conventions, weakening fluency of writing
1	• Uses an ineffective organization for a persuasive essay • Does not convey ideas in a sustained, persuasive way • Has few or no transitions between ideas, sentences, and paragraphs	• Fails to state a thesis or support it with reasons and evidence • Fails to present other relevant perspectives • Uses few or no effective rhetorical devices or appeals to logic, emotions, and ethical beliefs	• Lacks appropriate word choice for form and purpose; has an inappropriate tone • Uses monotonously structured sentences that consistently lack purpose and control • Demonstrates limited knowledge of conventions

© Houghton Mifflin Harcourt Publishing Company

Benchmark Composition: Persuasive Essay 1   Score Point 2

Marble Not Music—Are You Kidding?

I understand that we all have to cut back. I used to download a lot more music than I do now. Getting rid of classes in art, music, and theater to save money is a bad idea. Why you ask? Well here are some reasons.

First of all our school wins alot of art awards. My oil painting of my dog won an honorable mention at a local art show. I was so exited that I decided rite then and there to be an art teacher. When we win awards our school gets good attention. That is way better than bad attention. Like for kids getting in trouble.

The school district could find other money. Think about it. Did the middle school really need a new marble floor in the lobby? I dont think so. It is a school, not a musuem. Dont tell me that didnt cost money. Because it did. We can have marble not music? Those priorities seem pretty wierd to me. Cut marble floors not classes.

DEVELOPMENT OF IDEAS
The writer establishes a definite position on the issue followed by two specific reasons. However, the writer fails to explain the significance of some of the ideas, which weakens the overall effectiveness of the editorial.

USE OF LANGUAGE CONVENTIONS
The writer has not edited very carefully. There are misspellings, errors in punctuation, and sentence fragments. These mistakes distract readers from the writer's argument.

Name _____ Date _____

This editorial addresses the prompt, presenting two strong reasons for not cutting the school's arts programs. However, the writer fails to establish connections between ideas. This lack of transitional words detracts from the logical progression of the argument and weakens its overall effectiveness. Finally, errors in language conventions weaken the argument's impact.

	ORGANIZATION/ PROGRESSION	DEVELOPMENT OF IDEAS	USE OF LANGUAGE CONVENTIONS
4	• Uses an effective organization for a persuasive essay that is skillfully structured to suit the purpose, audience, and context • Conveys ideas in a sustained, persuasive way • Uses clear transitions between ideas, sentences, and paragraphs	• Advances a clear thesis or position fully supported by logical reasons and reliable, relevant evidence, including facts, expert opinions, and/or quotations • Presents a full range of relevant perspectives • Uses effective rhetorical devices and appeals to logic, emotions, and ethical beliefs	• Shows strong understanding of appropriate word choice for the form, purpose, and tone of a persuasive essay • Uses purposeful, varied, and controlled sentences • Demonstrates consistent command of conventions so that writing is fluent and clear
3	• Uses a reasonably effective organization for a persuasive essay, with a structure appropriate to the purpose, audience, and context • Conveys ideas in a fairly sustained, persuasive way • Uses transitions between ideas, sentences, and paragraphs	• Advances a fairly clear thesis or position supported by logical reasons and reliable, relevant evidence • Presents a range of relevant perspectives • Uses rhetorical devices and appeals to logic, emotions, and ethical beliefs	• Shows basic understanding of word choice appropriate for a persuasive essay • Uses sentences that are purposeful, varied, and controlled for the most part • Demonstrates a good command of conventions; writing is mostly fluent and clear
2	• Uses a somewhat effective organization for a persuasive essay that shows some attention to purpose, audience, and context • Does not convey all ideas in a sustained, persuasive way • Uses too few transitions between ideas, sentences, and paragraphs	• Has an unclear thesis or position statement; thesis is supported by insufficient reasons and evidence • Presents few relevant perspectives other than the author's • Uses few rhetorical devices or appeals to logic, emotions, and ethical beliefs	• Shows some understanding of word choice; may be inappropriate to form, purpose, or tone • May use awkward, rambling sentences or unvaried sentence structure • Demonstrates limited command of conventions, weakening fluency of writing
1	• Uses an ineffective organization for a persuasive essay • Does not convey ideas in a sustained, persuasive way • Has few or no transitions between ideas, sentences, and paragraphs	• Fails to state a thesis or support it with reasons and evidence • Fails to present other relevant perspectives • Uses few or no effective rhetorical devices or appeals to logic, emotions, and ethical beliefs	• Lacks appropriate word choice for form and purpose; has an inappropriate tone • Uses monotonously structured sentences that consistently lack purpose and control • Demonstrates limited knowledge of conventions

© Houghton Mifflin Harcourt Publishing Company

Written Composition: Persuasive Essay 2

READ

Read the quotation in the box below.

> "We all participate in weaving the social fabric; we should therefore all participate in patching the fabric when it develops holes. . . ."
>
> *Anne C. Weisberg*

THINK

There are many social problems in today's world. Think of one that affects people around you, such as hunger, pollution, or violence. What can you and other individuals do to raise awareness of the issue and work toward a solution?

WRITE

Write a speech to be given at a school assembly in which you persuade your fellow students to participate in your plan for solving a problem.

As you write your composition, remember to —

☐ state a thesis that identifies your plan for solving a specific social problem

☐ organize the main points of your plan and supporting details logically and effectively

☐ develop your plan by describing the full extent of the problem and by supporting the solution with appropriate evidence and rhetorical devices that strengthen your assertions

☐ make sure your composition is no longer than one page

TEKS 13A, 13B, 13C, 13D, 16A, 16D, 16E, 17, 18, 19

ANALYZE THE PROMPT
The prompt asks you to write a speech identifying a social problem and persuading your fellow students to participate in your plan for a solution. You must clearly explain the problem, your position, and the details of your plan.

RESPOND TO THE PROMPT
- **Plan** by identifying possible social problems that have a local effect. Select the one that you feel most strongly about and have an idea for solving. Then identify facts, examples, and other details that support your plan.
- **Draft** your response by describing the problem and introducing your solution. Present the details of your solution in an order that makes sense.
- **Revise** to use more precise wording, to vary the lengths and variety of your sentences, and to add additional explanation and transitions.
- **Edit** your writing to correct any errors in spelling, grammar, punctuation, or capitalization.

Benchmark Composition: Persuasive Essay 2   Score Point 4

Waste Not, Want Not

Every day in the school parking lot, I have to wade through half-full bags of chips and uneaten pizza crusts. The littering is bad enough; the wasting of food is criminal. Americans are so used to living in the land of plenty that we feel we must have plenty all the time, even when we don't want it. We need to stop wasting food that could be given to the hungry in our community. I propose that we start right here in our school.

In the U.S., over forty percent of the food produced goes uneaten. This adds up to more than 29 million tons. On average, we throw out approximately 6,000 tons of food a day. Just think how many hungry people could benefit from this abundance if we had a system in place for collecting it.

We have put together such a system for our school. Maybe we won't save tons of food from being thrown out, but every little bit counts. In the next week, we are going to set up boxes throughout the school for food donations. If you have juice boxes, packaged cookies or crackers, or any other nonperishable items in your lunch that you don't eat, instead of tossing them out, place them in one of the boxes. At the end of each month, donate canned goods that your family won't eat. The contents of the food-donation boxes will be delivered right to our local food bank on a frequent basis.

Next to the cashier in the cafeteria, we will also have a container for change. As you go through the line, consciously decide against that extra hot dog that ends up left on the tray. Don't buy dessert. Instead of left-over food, you will have left-over cash that you can drop into the container. Our local shelter will use these donations to feed their residents.

When I was little, my mother would scold me for wasting food, saying that it could feed a starving child somewhere else. I usually snorted at the thought that my half-eaten burger could go to some hungry person six thousand miles away. But now I understand what she was trying to tell me. Taking just what I need ensures others get what they need.

So, as you go through the buffet line at your favorite restaurant, as you buy your lunch, as you bring in snacks for your club meeting, I would ask you to think twice about what you want, what you need, and what you may end up wasting. Wasting not can help someone else want not.

DEVELOPMENT OF IDEAS
The writer identifies a social problem about which she feels strongly and states her view on it. She uses parallelism to emphasize her point.

DEVELOPMENT OF IDEAS
The second paragraph develops the extent of the problem with facts and statistics that appeal to the audience's logic and ethical beliefs.

ORGANIZATION/ PROGRESSION
In the third paragraph, the writer begins the explanation of her action plan, presenting specific details including a time frame. Transitions such as *next to*, *also*, and *as* help the audience follow the progression of ideas.

DEVELOPMENT OF IDEAS
The writer includes an anecdote to catch the attention of the audience. The anecdote also reinforces the point about not wasting food that has been developed throughout the speech.

Name _____ Date _____

The writer begins this persuasive speech with a description of the effect of a social problem on her community. The writer then makes listeners aware of the extent of the problem before describing an action plan. The writer's solution is supported by specific details and is expressed in a way that is appropriate for the listening audience. The writing contains no distracting errors.

	ORGANIZATION/ PROGRESSION	DEVELOPMENT OF IDEAS	USE OF LANGUAGE CONVENTIONS
4	• Uses an effective organization for a persuasive essay that is skillfully structured to suit the purpose, audience, and context • Conveys ideas in a sustained, persuasive way • Uses clear transitions between ideas, sentences, and paragraphs	• Advances a clear thesis or position fully supported by logical reasons and reliable, relevant evidence, including facts, expert opinions, and/or quotations • Presents a full range of relevant perspectives • Uses effective rhetorical devices and appeals to logic, emotions, and ethical beliefs	• Shows strong understanding of appropriate word choice for the form, purpose, and tone of a persuasive essay • Uses purposeful, varied, and controlled sentences • Demonstrates consistent command of conventions so that writing is fluent and clear
3	• Uses a reasonably effective organization for a persuasive essay, with a structure appropriate to the purpose, audience, and context • Conveys ideas in a fairly sustained, persuasive way • Uses transitions between ideas, sentences, and paragraphs	• Advances a fairly clear thesis or position supported by logical reasons and reliable, relevant evidence • Presents a range of relevant perspectives • Uses rhetorical devices and appeals to logic, emotions, and ethical beliefs	• Shows basic understanding of word choice appropriate for a persuasive essay • Uses sentences that are purposeful, varied, and controlled for the most part • Demonstrates a good command of conventions; writing is mostly fluent and clear
2	• Uses a somewhat effective organization for a persuasive essay that shows some attention to purpose, audience, and context • Does not convey all ideas in a sustained, persuasive way • Uses too few transitions between ideas, sentences, and paragraphs	• Has an unclear thesis or position statement; thesis is supported by insufficient reasons and evidence • Presents few relevant perspectives other than the author's • Uses few rhetorical devices or appeals to logic, emotions, and ethical beliefs	• Shows some understanding of word choice; may be inappropriate to form, purpose, or tone • May use awkward, rambling sentences or unvaried sentence structure • Demonstrates limited command of conventions, weakening fluency of writing
1	• Uses an ineffective organization for a persuasive essay • Does not convey ideas in a sustained, persuasive way • Has few or no transitions between ideas, sentences, and paragraphs	• Fails to state a thesis or support it with reasons and evidence • Fails to present other relevant perspectives • Uses few or no effective rhetorical devices or appeals to logic, emotions, and ethical beliefs	• Lacks appropriate word choice for form and purpose; has an inappropriate tone • Uses monotonously structured sentences that consistently lack purpose and control • Demonstrates limited knowledge of conventions

© Houghton Mifflin Harcourt Publishing Company

Benchmark Composition: Persuasive Essay 2   Score Point 2

R-E-S-P-E-C-T—Just a Little Bit

There is no respect for other people's property anymore. Last week, all of my neighbors woke up to find eggs covering their cars, it was so hot that the eggs had almost baked on. Cleaning them off removed the finish too. Since when did destruction of property become the new pastime? We see it in our school too. Graffiti is all over. Not the creative kind either. Kids randomly break lockers and equipment for fun. We need to start showing respect for our environment. We need to begin right here.

Maybe when you were in grade school, it was bad to tattle tale, now it isn't. If you see someone defacing property on the school grounds. Do one of two things. Take a picture of the culprit with your phone, show it to an administrator or member of my committee. Or, call the number on the screen in back of me. Someone will respond.

If everyone looks the other way, the problem will continue. Lack of respect for property equals lack of respect for others.

DEVELOPMENT OF IDEAS
The first paragraph clearly identifies a social problem that is affecting local neighborhoods as well as the school. The writer suggests a solution but fails to provide enough details to fully explain the plan.

USE OF LANGUAGE CONVENTIONS
The writer's vocabulary and spelling are both excellent. However, many run-on sentences and some sentence fragments show a lack of understanding of basic sentence structure.

Persuasive Essay 2: Score Summary and Rubric   **Score Point 2**

In this speech, the writer states a clear problem and its effects. The solution however, is poorly developed. Few specific details are given to explain who is in charge of responding, other measures that will be taken to prevent vandalism, and the penalty for those caught destroying property. The many grammatical errors also distract from the fluency of the speech.

	ORGANIZATION/ PROGRESSION	DEVELOPMENT OF IDEAS	USE OF LANGUAGE CONVENTIONS
4	• Uses an effective organization for a persuasive essay that is skillfully structured to suit the purpose, audience, and context • Conveys ideas in a sustained, persuasive way • Uses clear transitions between ideas, sentences, and paragraphs	• Advances a clear thesis or position fully supported by logical reasons and reliable, relevant evidence, including facts, expert opinions, and/or quotations • Presents a full range of relevant perspectives • Uses effective rhetorical devices and appeals to logic, emotions, and ethical beliefs	• Shows strong understanding of appropriate word choice for the form, purpose, and tone of a persuasive essay • Uses purposeful, varied, and controlled sentences • Demonstrates consistent command of conventions so that writing is fluent and clear
3	• Uses a reasonably effective organization for a persuasive essay, with a structure appropriate to the purpose, audience, and context • Conveys ideas in a fairly sustained, persuasive way • Uses transitions between ideas, sentences, and paragraphs	• Advances a fairly clear thesis or position supported by logical reasons and reliable, relevant evidence • Presents a range of relevant perspectives • Uses rhetorical devices and appeals to logic, emotions, and ethical beliefs	• Shows basic understanding of word choice appropriate for a persuasive essay • Uses sentences that are purposeful, varied, and controlled for the most part • Demonstrates a good command of conventions; writing is mostly fluent and clear
2	• Uses a somewhat effective organization for a persuasive essay that shows some attention to purpose, audience, and context • Does not convey all ideas in a sustained, persuasive way • Uses too few transitions between ideas, sentences, and paragraphs	• Has an unclear thesis or position statement; thesis is supported by insufficient reasons and evidence • Presents few relevant perspectives other than the author's • Uses few rhetorical devices or appeals to logic, emotions, and ethical beliefs	• Shows some understanding of word choice; may be inappropriate to form, purpose, or tone • May use awkward, rambling sentences or unvaried sentence structure • Demonstrates limited command of conventions, weakening fluency of writing
1	• Uses an ineffective organization for a persuasive essay • Does not convey ideas in a sustained, persuasive way • Has few or no transitions between ideas, sentences, and paragraphs	• Fails to state a thesis or support it with reasons and evidence • Fails to present other relevant perspectives • Uses few or no effective rhetorical devices or appeals to logic, emotions, and ethical beliefs	• Lacks appropriate word choice for form and purpose; has an inappropriate tone • Uses monotonously structured sentences that consistently lack purpose and control • Demonstrates limited knowledge of conventions

© Houghton Mifflin Harcourt Publishing Company

Written Composition: Expository Essay 1

READ

Read the quotation in the box below.

> "Make the most of today. Get interested in something. Shake yourself awake. Develop a hobby. . . . Live today with gusto."
>
> *Dale Carnegie*

THINK

Think about hobbies or pastimes that you have. Which do you find especially enjoyable? Why? Consider what is most satisfying about your favorite hobbies.

WRITE

Write an expository essay that explains why you find a hobby or activity enjoyable.

As you write your composition, remember to —

☐ develop a thesis statement that explains why your hobby or activity is interesting

☐ organize your ideas in a logical order and connect them with appropriate transitions

☐ develop your ideas fully and thoughtfully with well-chosen details and precise words

☐ make sure your composition is no longer than one page

TEKS 13A, 13B, 13C, 13D, 15A, 17, 18, 19

ANALYZE THE PROMPT
The prompt asks you to explain what makes a hobby interesting or enjoyable to you. This means you should clearly state what you like most about your hobby and then provide details and examples to support your thesis.

RESPOND TO THE PROMPT
- **Plan** by listing your hobbies. Identify your favorite part of each one. Choose the hobby that you enjoy most or do most frequently.
- **Draft** your response by writing an introduction that states your thesis. Then write one or more paragraphs that support your thesis with details and examples. End with a conclusion that restates your thesis in a powerful way.
- **Revise** to use more precise wording, to vary your sentence types, and to add transitions connecting ideas.
- **Edit** your essay to correct any remaining errors in spelling, grammar, punctuation, and capitalization.

Benchmark Composition: Expository Essay 1

Score Point 4

Exploring the Night Sky

Stargazing is a fascinating hobby. The wonders of the universe are waiting to be observed in the night sky, but our eyes are not powerful enough to capture the light we need to fully see these objects. Telescopes are designed to collect an amount of light many times greater than the amount the naked eye can gather. For me, the challenge of working with such precise instruments and choosing the right one for my purpose is one of the most absorbing parts of my pastime.

The oldest and most common telescope available is a refractor telescope. The refractor uses a big lens at the front to bend, or refract, light to a focus. When I first began my stargazing, I purchased a refractor because this type of telescope provides crisp images. It is ideal for viewing the moon and other planetary objects. It also has the advantage of requiring little maintenance. However, refractor telescopes have the disadvantage that they cannot collect enough light to allow viewing of deep-space objects outside our solar system.

After I became more serious about my hobby, I acquired a second telescope commonly called a reflector. A reflector telescope uses a large curved mirror instead of a lens to gather and focus light. These simple yet high-quality telescopes deliver bright images. They are ideal for viewing deep-sky objects such as galaxies, nebulae, and star clusters. Reflectors are somewhat fragile, however, and they require regular maintenance for the best possible images.

I am hoping one day to get the most recently developed telescope available, which is the catadioptric, or compound, telescope. This uses both lenses and mirrors to gather and focus light in a compact tube. Catadioptric telescopes have some special options, such as advanced tracking and electronics that allow users to locate sky targets reliably. However, they cost more than comparable reflectors, the focusing mechanism can be imprecise, and the scope can be taken apart only by the manufacturer. Maybe if I wait long enough, these drawbacks will be eliminated.

My first piece of equipment was actually a pair of binoculars. These binoculars, although lacking the features of my later telescopes, opened up a new world to me. I knew right then that with the right tools my viewing possibilities would be truly astronomical!

ORGANIZATION/ PROGRESSION
A strong thesis clearly identifies what aspect of stargazing the writer finds most enjoyable and why.

DEVELOPMENT OF IDEAS
The writer explains the advantages and disadvantages of each type of telescope, helping readers understand what makes each unique and why a serious stargazer would need more than one instrument.

ORGANIZATION/ PROGRESSION
The writer's frequent use of transitions—such as *after, instead of,* and *however*—helps readers follow the progression of ideas and signals the relationships among details.

DEVELOPMENT OF IDEAS
The conclusion, although brief, provides insight into how the writer's fascination with instruments and stargazing began.

Expository Essay 1: Score Summary and Rubric   **Score Point 4**

This expository essay views the prompt from an unexpected angle, since readers are not expecting the telescopes to be what is most fascinating about stargazing. Through the writer's specific details, however, readers begin to understand the source of this enthusiasm. The writer uses a variety of sentence structures and shows a strong command of conventions.

	ORGANIZATION/ PROGRESSION	DEVELOPMENT OF IDEAS	USE OF LANGUAGE CONVENTIONS
4	• Uses appropriate structure for purpose and demands of the prompt • Establishes and sustains focus, unity, and coherence via the thesis • Controls progression with transitions showing relationships among ideas	• Employs specific and well-chosen details and examples • Engages the reader through thoughtful development of ideas; may approach topic from an unusual perspective; demonstrates a deep understanding of prompt	• Shows understanding of word choice appropriate to purpose and intended tone • Uses purposeful, varied, and controlled sentences • Demonstrates a command of conventions so that essay is rhetorically effective even if it contains minor errors
3	• Uses mostly effective structure for purpose and demands of prompt • Relates most ideas to thesis; essay is coherent though may lack overall unity • Mostly controls progression of ideas with transitions	• Employs specific, appropriate details and examples that add some substance to essay • Demonstrates some depth of thought, with an original rather than formulaic approach, and a good understanding of the task	• Shows a basic understanding of word choice appropriate to purpose and intended tone • Uses varied and generally controlled sentences • Demonstrates general command of conventions; errors do not seriously affect clarity or fluency
2	• May use structure that is inappropriate to prompt; structure may not contribute to clarity of explanation • May use weak or unclear thesis, reducing focus and coherence • Has inconsistent progression of thought, with too few meaningful transitions and connections	• Lacks strong development of ideas because details are inappropriate or insufficiently developed • Demonstrates little depth of thought, with a formulaic approach to the prompt and a limited understanding of the task	• Shows limited grasp of word choice, failing to establish appropriate tone • Uses awkward or uncontrolled sentences, weakening essay's effectiveness • Demonstrates partial command of conventions; errors may result in a lack of fluency or clarity
1	• Uses inappropriate or no obvious structure • Lacks clear thesis, with resulting weak focus and coherence • Has weak progression of thought, with lack of meaningful transitions and connections among ideas	• Lacks strong development of ideas because details and examples are inappropriate, vague, or insufficient • Demonstrates lack of understanding of prompt through an overall insubstantial essay and/or a vague or confused approach	• Lacks understanding of word choice; vocabulary is imprecise or unsuitable • Uses simplistic, awkward, or uncontrolled sentences, weakening essay's effectiveness • Demonstrates limited or no command of conventions, resulting in a lack of fluency

© Houghton Mifflin Harcourt Publishing Company

Benchmark Composition: Expository Essay 1 Score Point 2

A Sweet Hobby

In my day, I have enjoyed some grate hobbies. For example, when I was young. I was a balet dancer. When I was older I rode horses. But, I really love making up cakes. I love changing recipes. To see if I can make them better.

Usally I find a basic recipe, like for a white or a chocalate cake. Then I think about other flavors that could be added. I decide if I want to put in fruit. I use bananas a lot and peaches. My brother loves bananas. Or some kind of candy or nut. Some people are alergic to nuts, but I'm not. Then I make it. Sometimes people like it. Sometimes they don't. I don't care. I do it for me mostly. I try to write down what I use. So that I can make the same cake again if it's good. Last weeks wasn't so good. My spicey chocalate cake came out tasting like a chili burger. Yuck! I guess I won't be making that again.

Maybe next year I will have a different hobby. For now I am happy in the kitchen. Making my cakes. And eating them too!

DEVELOPMENT OF IDEAS
This writer has interpreted the prompt well and includes some specific details in support of the thesis stated at the end of the first paragraph. However, several ideas are irrelevant, resulting in an essay that is disorganized and weak.

USE OF LANGUAGE CONVENTIONS
Misspellings and grammatical errors, such as sentence fragments, make the essay difficult to read.

Expository Essay 1: Score Summary and Rubric   **Score Point 2**

This expository essay clearly identifies a specific aspect of a hobby that the writer finds enjoyable. Strong details launch the second paragraph. However, the order and relevance of the details deteriorate by the middle of the essay. In addition, the numerous errors in language conventions make the essay hard to read and appreciate.

	ORGANIZATION/ PROGRESSION	DEVELOPMENT OF IDEAS	USE OF LANGUAGE CONVENTIONS
4	• Uses appropriate structure for purpose and demands of the prompt • Establishes and sustains focus, unity, and coherence via the thesis • Controls progression with transitions showing relationships among ideas	• Employs specific and well-chosen details and examples • Engages the reader through thoughtful development of ideas; may approach topic from an unusual perspective; demonstrates a deep understanding of prompt	• Shows understanding of word choice appropriate to purpose and intended tone • Uses purposeful, varied, and controlled sentences • Demonstrates a command of conventions so that essay is rhetorically effective even if it contains minor errors
3	• Uses mostly effective structure for purpose and demands of prompt • Relates most ideas to thesis; essay is coherent though may lack overall unity • Mostly controls progression of ideas with transitions	• Employs specific, appropriate details and examples that add some substance to essay • Demonstrates some depth of thought, with an original rather than formulaic approach, and a good understanding of the task	• Shows a basic understanding of word choice appropriate to purpose and intended tone • Uses varied and generally controlled sentences • Demonstrates general command of conventions; errors do not seriously affect clarity or fluency
2	• May use structure that is inappropriate to prompt; structure may not contribute to clarity of explanation • May use weak or unclear thesis, reducing focus and coherence • Has inconsistent progression of thought, with too few meaningful transitions and connections	• Lacks strong development of ideas because details are inappropriate or insufficiently developed • Demonstrates little depth of thought, with a formulaic approach to the prompt and a limited understanding of the task	• Shows limited grasp of word choice, failing to establish appropriate tone • Uses awkward or uncontrolled sentences, weakening essay's effectiveness • Demonstrates partial command of conventions; errors may result in a lack of fluency or clarity
1	• Uses inappropriate or no obvious structure • Lacks clear thesis, with resulting weak focus and coherence • Has weak progression of thought, with lack of meaningful transitions and connections among ideas	• Lacks strong development of ideas because details and examples are inappropriate, vague, or insufficient • Demonstrates lack of understanding of prompt through an overall insubstantial essay and/or a vague or confused approach	• Lacks understanding of word choice; vocabulary is imprecise or unsuitable • Uses simplistic, awkward, or uncontrolled sentences, weakening essay's effectiveness • Demonstrates limited or no command of conventions, resulting in a lack of fluency

Written Composition: Expository Essay 2

READ

Read the quotation in the box below.

> "You can fall in love at first sight with a place as with a person."
>
> *Alec Waugh*

THINK

Think about a place that you love. It might be your own town or city or a special vacation spot. What makes this location unique? What are its distinctive features or interesting sights?

WRITE

Write an expository essay that explains the attractions of a particular place, either your own town or city or somewhere else that you have visited.

As you write your composition, remember to —

☐ state a thesis that explains the outstanding features of the location you have chosen

☐ organize your ideas in a logical order and connect them with appropriate transitions

☐ develop your ideas fully and thoughtfully with well-chosen details and precise words

☐ make sure your composition is no longer than one page

TEKS 13A, 13B, 13C, 13D, 15A, 17, 18, 19

ANALYZE THE PROMPT
The prompt asks you to explain why you love a particular place. This means you should clearly state its major attractions and then provide details and facts that support your thesis.

RESPOND TO THE PROMPT
- **Plan** by listing your favorite places. Identify what makes each one special to you. Choose the location that you feel most strongly about or that has the most unique features.
- **Draft** your response by writing an introduction that states your thesis. Then write one or more paragraphs that support your thesis with details and examples. End with a conclusion that restates your thesis in a powerful way.
- **Revise** to use more precise wording, to vary your sentence types, and to add transitions connecting ideas.
- **Edit** your essay to correct any remaining errors in spelling, grammar, punctuation, and capitalization.

Benchmark Composition: Expository Essay 2   Score Point 4

The Wonders of Watkins Glen

When my parents first told me that we were taking a trip to Watkins Glen in upstate New York, I was less than enthusiastic. Apparently my mother had some conference to attend there and decided to drag us all along. I vaguely recognized the name from car racing events, but I couldn't imagine what was in it for me! That was my feeling before we arrived. However, as soon as we drove down the main street of Watkins Glen in our rental car, I fell in love. This small village, easily navigated on foot, is surrounded by scenic hills, bordered by majestic gorges, and nestled at the foot of one of the loveliest Finger Lakes. For someone who appreciates natural beauty and enjoys outdoor activities, it is a Shangri-La!

Just off the main street, within walking distance of the hotels and motels, is the Watkins Glen State Park. For no admission fee, visitors can spend the day or several days hiking trails that curve along the edges of steep cliffs and sheer drops and behind magnificent waterfalls. There are dangling suspension bridges—not for the faint of heart!—unusual rock formations, wild scenery, and plenty of opportunities for the obligatory vacation photographs. Plaques posted along the way share facts about the foliage and other features of the landscape. When you are tired, your hotel is just a short stroll away from the entrance.

Seneca Lake offers an even greater range of enjoyable activities. There are cruises, sailboats to rent, and all sorts of water activities. Beware—Seneca Lake is very deep, so the water will be either refreshing or icy, depending on your perspective! You can take a short boat tour to learn about the salt mines deep below the lake that are still being worked today as well as the first inhabitants of the area, from whom the name Seneca is taken. From the middle of the lake, you get a great view of the houses scattered along the shore, sheltered by densely wooded hills rising up behind them. After your ride, there are plenty of places to sit and gaze at the sparkling water.

Our time in Watkins Glen came to an end all too soon. When we left, part of my heart remained. To me, that location offers everything that any lover of the outdoors could ever want. Watkins Glen truly is "gorge-ous"!

DEVELOPMENT OF IDEAS
The opening sentences capture the reader's attention by describing the writer's initial reaction to Watkins Glen. The writer ends the first paragraph with a clear thesis statement that responds directly to the prompt.

ORGANIZATION/ PROGRESSION
In the body paragraphs, the writer explains the two major attractions of Watkins Glen, the state park and the lake, presenting details that show why each feature is unique.

ORGANIZATION/ PROGRESSION
Throughout the essay, the writer uses transitions that indicate spatial and chronological relationships among the ideas.

DEVELOPMENT OF IDEAS
In the conclusion, the writer restates the thesis and finishes with a memorable and enthusiastic tribute to Watkins Glen.

© Houghton Mifflin Harcourt Publishing Company

Expository Essay 2: Score Summary and Rubric

This expository essay addresses the prompt directly and fully, explaining the two major features of Watkins Glen that the writer finds most interesting and unique. The details all support the thesis, and the informative yet personal tone conveys the writer's positive feelings for the place. The writer uses a variety of sentence structures and shows a strong command of conventions.

	ORGANIZATION/ PROGRESSION	DEVELOPMENT OF IDEAS	USE OF LANGUAGE CONVENTIONS
4	• Uses appropriate structure for purpose and demands of the prompt • Establishes and sustains focus, unity, and coherence via the thesis • Controls progression with transitions showing relationships among ideas	• Employs specific and well-chosen details and examples • Engages the reader through thoughtful development of ideas; may approach topic from an unusual perspective; demonstrates a deep understanding of prompt	• Shows understanding of word choice appropriate to purpose and intended tone • Uses purposeful, varied, and controlled sentences • Demonstrates a command of conventions so that essay is rhetorically effective even if it contains minor errors
3	• Uses mostly effective structure for purpose and demands of prompt • Relates most ideas to thesis; essay is coherent though may lack overall unity • Mostly controls progression of ideas with transitions	• Employs specific, appropriate details and examples that add some substance to essay • Demonstrates some depth of thought, with an original rather than formulaic approach, and a good understanding of the task	• Shows a basic understanding of word choice appropriate to purpose and intended tone • Uses varied and generally controlled sentences • Demonstrates general command of conventions; errors do not seriously affect clarity or fluency
2	• May use structure that is inappropriate to prompt; structure may not contribute to clarity of explanation • May use weak or unclear thesis, reducing focus and coherence • Has inconsistent progression of thought, with too few meaningful transitions and connections	• Lacks strong development of ideas because details are inappropriate or insufficiently developed • Demonstrates little depth of thought, with a formulaic approach to the prompt and a limited understanding of the task	• Shows limited grasp of word choice, failing to establish appropriate tone • Uses awkward or uncontrolled sentences, weakening essay's effectiveness • Demonstrates partial command of conventions; errors may result in a lack of fluency or clarity
1	• Uses inappropriate or no obvious structure • Lacks clear thesis, with resulting weak focus and coherence • Has weak progression of thought, with lack of meaningful transitions and connections among ideas	• Lacks strong development of ideas because details and examples are inappropriate, vague, or insufficient • Demonstrates lack of understanding of prompt through an overall insubstantial essay and/or a vague or confused approach	• Lacks understanding of word choice; vocabulary is imprecise or unsuitable • Uses simplistic, awkward, or uncontrolled sentences, weakening essay's effectiveness • Demonstrates limited or no command of conventions, resulting in a lack of fluency

Name _____ Date _____

Benchmark Composition: Expository Essay 2   **Score Point 2**

My Neighborhood

I love my neighborhood the most. To others it may seem pretty ordinary. To me it is pretty special.

I walk in Jack's Grocery Store. I smell spilled coffee beans. I smell some kind of spice in the air. I could know where I was even with a blind fold on. I pick up some groceries for my mom. Jack always knows what she wants. Jack's brother is my father's best friend. They grew up together. They still see each other almost every day. Next door is Angie's Pizzeria. We go there every Friday night for dinner. We know everybody. Everybody knows us. Her recipe for sauce is amazing. It is sweet but not too sweet. At the end of the street is my house. It is in the middle of three houses. They all look alike. My aunt lives in one. My best friend lives in the other one. So we are like one big happy family. My neighborhood is not exciting. It is not glamorous. It is not even interesting. But I love it.

DEVELOPMENT OF IDEAS
The first paragraph clearly identifies the writer's thesis. The body of the essay, however, fails to follow through. Irrelevant details create confusion, and there are no transitions to show how the relevant details relate to each other. The writer also does not explain the significance of the ideas presented.

USE OF LANGUAGE CONVENTIONS
There are few grammatical or spelling errors. However, the repetition of simple sentences creates a choppy and monotonous effect.

Expository Essay 2: Score Summary and Rubric **Score Point 2**

This expository essay shows some understanding of the prompt but fails to develop the thesis with adequate details. The writer does not explain the significance of the ideas that are presented or connect them with transitions. The essay's logical progression is interrupted by irrelevant observations. The writer uses only short, simple sentences, creating a choppy effect.

	ORGANIZATION/ PROGRESSION	DEVELOPMENT OF IDEAS	USE OF LANGUAGE CONVENTIONS
4	• Uses appropriate structure for purpose and demands of the prompt • Establishes and sustains focus, unity, and coherence via the thesis • Controls progression with transitions showing relationships among ideas	• Employs specific and well-chosen details and examples • Engages the reader through thoughtful development of ideas; may approach topic from an unusual perspective; demonstrates a deep understanding of prompt	• Shows understanding of word choice appropriate to purpose and intended tone • Uses purposeful, varied, and controlled sentences • Demonstrates a command of conventions so that essay is rhetorically effective even if it contains minor errors
3	• Uses mostly effective structure for purpose and demands of prompt • Relates most ideas to thesis; essay is coherent though may lack overall unity • Mostly controls progression of ideas with transitions	• Employs specific, appropriate details and examples that add some substance to essay • Demonstrates some depth of thought, with an original rather than formulaic approach, and a good understanding of the task	• Shows a basic understanding of word choice appropriate to purpose and intended tone • Uses varied and generally controlled sentences • Demonstrates general command of conventions; errors do not seriously affect clarity or fluency
2	• May use structure that is inappropriate to prompt; structure may not contribute to clarity of explanation • May use weak or unclear thesis, reducing focus and coherence • Has inconsistent progression of thought, with too few meaningful transitions and connections	• Lacks strong development of ideas because details are inappropriate or insufficiently developed • Demonstrates little depth of thought, with a formulaic approach to the prompt and a limited understanding of the task	• Shows limited grasp of word choice, failing to establish appropriate tone • Uses awkward or uncontrolled sentences, weakening essay's effectiveness • Demonstrates partial command of conventions; errors may result in a lack of fluency or clarity
1	• Uses inappropriate or no obvious structure • Lacks clear thesis, with resulting weak focus and coherence • Has weak progression of thought, with lack of meaningful transitions and connections among ideas	• Lacks strong development of ideas because details and examples are inappropriate, vague, or insufficient • Demonstrates lack of understanding of prompt through an overall insubstantial essay and/or a vague or confused approach	• Lacks understanding of word choice; vocabulary is imprecise or unsuitable • Uses simplistic, awkward, or uncontrolled sentences, weakening essay's effectiveness • Demonstrates limited or no command of conventions, resulting in a lack of fluency

© Houghton Mifflin Harcourt Publishing Company

Written Composition Practice: Persuasive Essay 1

READ

Read the quotation in the box below.

> "Even when laws have been written down, they ought not always to remain unaltered."
>
> *Aristotle*

THINK

Consider the various rules of your school. Some govern your behavior, some ensure your safety and well-being, and others establish procedures. Are there any that you think should be changed or eliminated? Would you like to see a rule added?

WRITE

Write an editorial for the school newspaper that argues for a rule to be changed, dropped, or added.

As you write your composition, remember to —

☐ craft a thesis that clearly states why you would like a rule added, changed, or eliminated

☐ organize your reasons and supporting evidence logically and effectively

☐ develop your argument with strong reasons supported by facts, examples, description, and other relevant details

☐ make sure your composition is no longer than one page

Written Composition Practice: Persuasive Essay 2

READ

Read the quotation in the box below.

> "It has become appallingly obvious that our technology has exceeded our humanity."
>
> *Albert Einstein*

THINK

Since Einstein's time, technology has become an even greater part of our daily lives. Is that a good thing, or has our dependence on technology harmed us?

WRITE

Write a persuasive essay for your local newspaper in which you argue whether the impact of technology on our society or on your life is beneficial or harmful. Include specific examples of technology to illustrate your point.

As you write your composition, remember to —

☐ craft a thesis that clearly states your position on the effect of technology on your life or on society in general

☐ organize your reasons and supporting evidence logically and effectively

☐ develop your argument with appropriate evidence and rhetorical devices to strengthen your assertions

☐ make sure your composition is no longer than one page

Written Composition Practice: Expository Essay 1

READ

Read the quotation in the box below.

> "Close your eyes and tap your heels together three times. And think to yourself, there's no place like home."
>
> from *The Wizard of Oz*

THINK

The word *home* conjures up different images for everyone who hears it. What is home to you? Is it the physical structure you live in? Or, does home mean the people with whom you share the important experiences of your life?

WRITE

Write an expository essay that defines the concept of "home." Include specific characteristics to support your definition.

As you write your composition, remember to —

☐ state a thesis that explains what "home" is

☐ organize your ideas in a logical order, using transitions to show the connections between ideas

☐ develop your ideas fully and thoughtfully with well-chosen details and precise words

☐ make sure your composition is no longer than one page

Written Composition Practice: Expository Essay 2

READ

Read the quotation in the box below.

> "An apple a day keeps the doctor away."
>
> *Unknown*

THINK

We know a little more about preventing illness than people did when this saying originated. However, the basic idea is sound—including fruit in your diet can contribute to good health. What are some other steps you can take to "keep the doctor away"?

WRITE

Write an expository essay that explains ways to stay healthy and prevent illness. Include at least two specific preventive or proactive measures.

As you write your composition, remember to —

☐ craft a thesis statement that identifies how certain actions or habits can contribute to overall health

☐ organize your ideas in a logical order, using transitions to show the connections between ideas

☐ develop your ideas fully and thoughtfully with well-chosen details and precise words

☐ make sure your composition is no longer than one page

Revising and Editing

Guided Revising

Read the following essay. Then read each question and mark the correct answer.

Antoine wrote this biographical essay about a major historical figure. He would like you to read his essay and think about improvements he should make. When you finish reading, answer the questions that follow.

Edward H. White: A Profile in Courage

(1) When President John F. Kennedy announced in 1962 that the United States would reach the moon by the end of the decade, no one knew how to do it. (2) Only years of determined effort and remarkable courage on the part of many scientists and astronauts could make this dream a reality. (3) One of those astronauts was Edward Higgins White II.

(4) Ed White was born on November 14, 1930, in San Antonio, Texas. (5) After graduating from the U.S. Military Academy at West Point, Ed enlisted in the Air Force and spent over three years flying jet fighters. (6) Then, in 1957, he read an article. (7) It changed his life. (8) Ed knew he wanted to do this, too, and he turned all his attention to pursuing a career as an astronaut.

(9) Ed earned a master's degree in aeronautical engineering and then enrolled in the Air Force Test Pilot School. (10) The space program began recruiting for its next project, and Ed was ready. (11) From over two hundred qualified applicants, he was one of nine test pilots chosen for Project Gemini, the second U.S.-manned space program.

(12) After months of astronaut training, Ed was selected as a pilot for the Gemini 4 mission. (13) The spacecraft would spend four days in orbit, and Ed would be the first American to "walk" outside the craft. (14) He would use a newly designed jet propulsion unit to maneuver himself through space. (15) Until ten days before take-off, the self-propulsion equipment was not even approved for use in space. (16) Ed was indeed brave to put his life on the line to test this new technology!

(17) Ed's space walk on June 3, 1965, was a triumph. (18) For his next mission, Apollo 1, he was promoted to Senior Pilot. (19) Sadly, this mission did not make it into space. (20) During a test on the launch pad, the command module caught fire, and Ed and two other astronauts died. (21) Ed was buried at West Point Cemetery and awarded the Congressional Space Medal of Honor in 1997. (22) All of them knew the risks of what they were doing, but they felt the risks were worth the dream of exploring space. (23) Their relentless courage and hard work have allowed others to achieve many dreams since their tragic death.

1 Antoine thinks sentences 6–7 sound choppy. What is the most effective way for him to combine them?

A Then, in 1957, he read an article, it changed his life.

B Then, in 1957, he read an article that changed his life.

C Then, in 1957, his life was changed by an article he read.

D Then, in 1957, he read an article, and this article changed his life.

> **EXPLANATION:** Antoine can combine the sentences clearly and concisely by using the relative pronoun *that* to change the second sentence to a relative clause. The correct answer is **B.**
> - **A** is incorrect because it is a run-on sentence.
> - **C** is incorrect. Using the passive voice ("his life was changed by") makes the sentence wordy and awkward.
> - **D** is incorrect because the sentence still sounds choppy with the repetition of the word *article.*

TEKS 13C

2 Antoine wants to help his audience understand Ed's decision to become an astronaut. Which sentence should Antoine add before sentence 8 to make his essay clear?

F The article appeared in a magazine about science and technology.

G The space program was the main topic of the article.

H Describing astronauts, the article was very interesting.

J The article described what astronauts would do in the future.

> **EXPLANATION:** It is unclear what *this* refers to in sentence 8. Readers need to know that the pronoun refers to what astronauts would do in the future. The correct answer is **J.**
> - **F, G,** and **H** are all incorrect. Each sentence provides more information about the article but doesn't tell what Ed wanted to do. None of these sentences makes sense placed in front of sentence 8.

TEKS 13C

GO ON →

3 To help readers follow the order of events in this essay, what is the most effective way for Antoine to revise sentence 10?

A When the space program began recruiting for its next project, Ed was ready.

B After the space program began, Ed was ready to be recruited for its next project.

C The space program began recruiting for its next project while Ed was ready.

D Recruitment for the space program's next project began, and this time Ed was ready.

EXPLANATION: The correct answer is **A**. The conjunction *when* creates a clear transition for the reader. The sentence explains that Ed was already prepared by the time the next project started.
- **B** is incorrect because it changes the meaning. The project was beginning, not the space program itself.
- **C** is incorrect. The conjunction *while* suggests a period of time rather than a specific moment, making the sequence of events less clear.
- **D** is incorrect because "this time Ed was ready" implies there was another time when he wasn't ready, but this is not discussed in the essay.

TEKS 13C

4 Which sentence should be removed from the last paragraph to make the conclusion more effective?

F Sentence 17
G Sentence 18
H Sentence 21
J Sentence 23

EXPLANATION: The paragraph focuses on the Apollo mission and the courage and sacrifice of the crew. Sentence 21 does not support the paragraph and causes confusion about the use of *them, they,* and *their* in the following sentences. **H** is correct.
- **F** is incorrect because sentence 17 provides a transition from the preceding paragraph.
- **G** and **J** are incorrect because they relate to and support the paragraph's main idea.

TEKS 13C

STOP

Name _____ Date _____

Revising Practice 1

Read the following essay. Then read each question and mark the correct answer.

Alexis wrote this essay about animal welfare organizations in the United States. She would like you to read her essay and think about the improvements she should make. When you finish reading, answer the questions that follow.

Animal Welfare Organizations

(1) The American Society for the Prevention of Cruelty to Animals (ASPCA) is the oldest animal welfare organization in the United States. (2) With the mission to "provide effective means for the prevention of cruelty to animals throughout the United States," it was founded in 1866. (3) Today, hundreds of such organizations operate at the local, state, and national levels to provide animal rescue services and to protect animals from cruelty, exploitation, and neglect.

(4) Most animal welfare organizations focus their efforts on rescuing and providing care to animals in need. (5) This may entail helping an animal that is trapped somewhere or bringing a lost or stray animal to a shelter. (6) Once an animal's medical and basic care needs have been met, animal welfare workers try to connect the animal with its owner, if possible, or place it in adoption. (7) Due to a lack of space or resources, animal shelters are sometimes unable to provide care to lost or stray animals. (8) In these cases, the animals might be put to sleep in a manner that doesn't cause much pain and suffering.

(9) In order to identify animals in need, welfare organizations investigate cases of abuse and neglect against animals. (10) In addition, animal rights workers seek to make sure that anti-cruelty regulations are followed by breeders, farmers, and researchers. (11) Acts of cruelty involving public exhibition such as dogfighting are another major area of concern.

(12) Animal welfare organizations also work for their cause by educating the public about important issues and by promoting community involvement. (13) Animal shelters encourage people to adopt animals in need of care. (14) Humane societies might also lead campaigns to outlaw harmful practices or change policies that hurt animals.

(15) Animal cruelty laws vary by state. (16) The Animal Welfare Act of 1966 is currently the only federal law that governs the treatment of animals by outlining standards for commercial breeding and transportation, research, and public exhibition. (17) The Animal Welfare Act is often cited as a basic guideline in other, more specific laws or policies.

GO ON

1 To better engage her readers and more clearly follow from sentence 1, what is the most effective way for Alexis to revise sentence 2?

A In 1866, its mission was to "provide effective means to prevent animal cruelty throughout the United States."

B Preventing animal cruelty was its mission when it was founded in 1866.

C Founding it in 1866 allowed its mission for preventing animal cruelty to develop.

D It was founded in 1866 with the mission to "provide effective means to prevent animal cruelty throughout the United States."

2 In sentence 6, Alexis thinks her description of the efforts to bring animals back to their owners sounds awkward. Which word is the most effective replacement for *connect*?

F Join

G Attach

H Reunite

J Transport

3 Alexis wants to provide more information to add to the ideas in the third paragraph (sentences 9–11). Which sentence could most logically follow sentence 9?

A This has only become common in recent years.

B Many organizations depend on private donations.

C Abuse and neglect are both very harmful to humans as well as animals.

D This often involves responding to calls from concerned citizens.

4 What transition word or phrase should Alexis insert at the beginning of sentence 13 to connect it with sentence 12?

F In fact

G However

H For example

J Nevertheless

5 Alexis notices that sentences 16 and 17 have almost the same beginning. To improve sentence variety, what is the most effective way to revise sentence 17?

A The act is often cited as a consequence of being a a guideline for other policies.

B Other, more specific laws or policies often refer to this law as a basic guideline.

C Often citing the act as a basic guideline is what more specific laws or policies do.

D References to the law as a basic guideline are often made in more specific laws or policies.

6 Alexis wants to conclude her essay with a statement that sums up the main idea for her audience. Which sentence should she add after sentence 17?

F Animal welfare organizations vary in their operating procedures, and some don't follow the Animal Welfare Act.

G Although animal welfare organizations operate under different laws, it is clear that they have come a long way since the founding of the ASPCA.

H The increase in the number of animal welfare organizations since 1866 is clearly a result of the differences in state laws.

J Regardless of differences in animal protection laws, all animal welfare organizations share a common mission to prevent cruelty and suffering.

Revising Practice 2

Read the following essay. Then read each question and mark the correct answer.

Sandra wrote this essay about ways to overcome a common fear. She wants you to read the essay and think about the improvements she should make. When you finish reading, answer the questions that follow.

Conquering the Fear of Public Speaking

(1) You all know the feeling: your knees shake, you sweat, your face changes color, and your stomach gets upset. (2) The reason is simple. (3) You're about to speak in front of a large group. (4) On the surface, it seems like a normal task. (5) For many of us, however, it can be a nightmare.

(6) I used to have a horrible fear of public speaking. (7) I would always try to stay away from those assignments. (8) My mother told me that public speaking builds self-confidence. (9) I disagreed, but it did not matter. (10) The assignments kept popping up!

(11) I decided to seek advice from our school's speech teacher, Mr. Rodriguez. (12) During our meeting I discovered that there are ways to overcome the fear of public speaking and become a confident speaker. (13) First, Mr. Rodriguez said that an effective speaker needs to look confident, no matter what he or she is feeling. (14) That meant speaking loudly and clearly. (15) I realized that if I thought about my voice, I would have less time to think about how frightened I was. (16) Next, he pointed out the need to make eye contact with the audience. (17) He knew that frightened speakers often look down at the floor, at the back of the room, or anywhere but at individual members of an audience. (18) He told me to practice looking directly at him while I was talking. (19) Then I practiced talking to the empty seats in the classroom, pretending the seats were filled with students and concentrating on each one. (20) Another strategy he encouraged was using gestures and body language effectively. (21) If you are thinking about gestures that go with your words, you even have less time to think about how nervous you are.

(22) After this interview, I learned two other steps in the process of overcoming the fear of public speaking. (23) These two steps in the process are important ones. (24) The first is to practice. (25) The second is to speak whenever you get the chance. (26) With experience, public speaking should become more natural and easy. (27) If you follow these tips, you too can conquer your fear of public speaking.

GO ON ➡️

1 Sandra wants to use figurative language to engage her audience in the opening. What is the most effective way for her to revise sentence 1?

  A We all know the feeling: your knees chatter, your skin feels clammy, your face turns red, and your stomach makes growling noises.

  B We all know the feeling: your knees shake like roosters, your palms get sweaty, your cheeks look like lemons, and your stomach gets angry.

  C We all know the feeling: your knees feel weak, you are drenched in sweat, your face feels strange, and churning stomach.

  D We all know the feeling: your knees begin to tremble, a bead of sweat trickles down your forehead, your cheeks ignite, and your stomach churns.

2 What is the most effective way for Sandra to revise sentence 7 so that its meaning in the paragraph is clear?

  F I would always get dreadfully nervous about speaking anywhere.

  G I would always rather listen to music or play sports than speak in front of an audience.

  H I would do anything to avoid assignments that involved speaking in front of the class.

  J I would choose assignments that involved an art project or doing something on the computer.

3 Sandra wants to add information to support the ideas in the second paragraph (sentences 6–10). Which sentence would be most effective to add after sentence 8?

  A I didn't see her doing much public speaking, though.

  B She also said public speaking is an important life skill.

  C I didn't want more self-confidence if that's what it would take.

  D She also suggested practicing more so it would get easier.

4 To highlight the importance of eye contact, Sandra wants to use a stronger verb in sentence 16. What is the most effective replacement for *pointed out*?

  F Implied

  G Accented

  H Embellished

  J Emphasized

GO ON

5 Sandra wants to add a personal example about gestures, as she did for the other two pieces of advice from Mr. Rodriguez. What would be the most effective sentence to add after sentence 21?

A It helps you feel more relaxed.

B Do you ever move your hands when you talk, as I do?

C It might sound difficult, but you can do it!

D I tried this a few times, and it really works!

6 How should Sandra combine sentences 22 and 23 to improve variety and conciseness?

F After this interview, I learned two other important steps in the process of overcoming the fear of public speaking.

G After this interview, I learned two other steps that are important in the process of overcoming the fear of public speaking.

H I learned two other steps after this interview in the process of overcoming the fear of public speaking: and both are important.

J I learned two other steps in the process of overcoming the fear of public speaking after this interview; both steps are important.

STOP

Guided Editing

Read the following narrative. Then read each question and mark the correct answer.

Sabrina wrote this personal narrative to describe her response to a major life event. She would like you to read her narrative and think about the corrections she should make. When you finish reading, answer the questions that follow.

Good-bye, Mexico!

(1) I looked at my father with an expression of horror on my face. (2) He explains that his company had awarded him a promotion with a new department, and we were moving from Mexico to the south of England in one month.

(3) "The weather is freezing in England," I grumbled.

(4) I was distraught, and I complained to anyone who would listen. (5) It was impossible imagine leaving the warm, humid Yucatán Peninsula. (6) I was positive that kids in England had never seen a surfboard. (7) How could my father ask me to give up the sport I loved?

(8) I told my father that moving to England was a horrible mistake.

(9) "England is a fantastic country," Dad said as he tried to reassure me.

(10) I walked into my room and rummaged through a drawer to find a stack of glossy photographs. (11) I looked at the picture of me fearlessly catching a gigantic wave last summer.

(12) My pitiful whining did not persuade my dad. (13) After packing up all of our belongings and flew to the southern coast of England. (14) As we traveled from the airport to our new home, I took a deep breath and exhaled loudly. (15) I realized that my former life was far away, and I had to accept it. (16) I gazed with disinterest at the picturesque landscape. (17) Suddenly, I noticed something amazing. (18) I peered out the window at the turbulent water. (19) I saw movement in an enormous wave. (20) I was filled with overwhelming joy! (21) "Dad, look. There is a surfer!" I exclaimed as I watched a girl swim ashore with a surfboard. (22) The look of melancholy on my face transformed into a radiant smile. (23) Maybe moving to England would be fantastic after all.

1 Which change should be made in sentence 2?

   A Delete the comma

   B Change *south* to **South**

   C Change *explains* to **explained**

   D Change *company* to **compeny**

> **EXPLANATION:** Verb tense should be consistent within a paragraph unless there is a valid reason for a shift. *Explains* is in the present tense, but the rest of the paragraph is in the past tense. The correct answer is **C**.
> - **A** is incorrect. The comma and coordinating conjunction are used correctly to join two independent clauses.
> - **B** is incorrect. Compass directions should not be capitalized unless they are used as part of a name.
> - **D** is incorrect because *company* is spelled correctly.

TEKS 13D, 17, 18, 19

2 What is the correct way to rewrite sentence 5?

   F It was impossible, imagine leaving the warm, humid Yucatán Peninsula.

   G It was impossible, imagine that I left the warm, humid Yucatán Peninsula.

   H It was impossible to imagine leaving the warm, humid Yucatán Peninsula.

   J It was impossible to imagine that I left the warm, humid Yucatán Peninsula.

> **EXPLANATION:** An infinitive (a verb form that usually begins with *to*) can act as a subject or its complement, a direct object, an adjective, or an adverb. In sentence 5, the infinitive phrase *to imagine leaving* completes, or complements, the subject *it* by telling what was impossible. The correct answer is **H**.
> - **F** and **G** are incorrect because they are run-ons—two complete sentences joined by a comma.
> - **J** is incorrect. The past tense should not be used in the second part of the sentence because Sabrina hasn't left yet—she is just grappling with the idea of having to do so.

TEKS 13D, 17, 18B

3 What is the correct way to rewrite sentence 13?

A We packed up all of our belongings, we flew to the southern coast of England.

B As we packed up all of our belongings, we flew to the southern coast of England.

C Once we packed up all of our belongings, we were flying to the southern coast of England.

D After packing up all of our belongings, we flew to the southern coast of England.

EXPLANATION: Complete sentences require a subject and a verb. The subject *we* is missing from sentence 13. The introductory phrase should be set off by a comma, and the conjunction *and* is not needed. The correct answer is **D**.

- **A** is incorrect because it is a run-on sentence.
- **B** is incorrect. The preposition *as* confuses the order of events by suggesting that the family packed and flew at the same time.
- **C** is incorrect. The past progressive tense of *were flying* is inconsistent with the rest of the narrative.

TEKS 13D, 17, 18B

4 What change, if any, should be made in sentence 14?

F Change *loudly* to **loud**

G Insert *and* after the comma

H Change *exhailed* to **exhaled**

J Make no change

EXPLANATION: The word *exhaled* is misspelled. The correct answer is **H**.

- **F** is incorrect. The adverb *loudly* correctly modifies the verb.
- **G** is incorrect. The clause *As we traveled from the airport to our new home* is a subordinate clause introducing a complex sentence, so the conjunction *and* is not appropriate.
- **J** is incorrect because a change is necessary to correct the spelling error.

TEKS 13D, 17C, 19

Editing Practice 1

Read the following personal narrative. Then read each question and mark the correct answer.

Ramón wrote this personal narrative to describe a source of influence in his life. He would like you to read his narrative and think about the corrections he should make. When you finish reading, answer the questions that follow.

How Cody Saved My Life

(1) The most important day of my life was the day which my service dog, Cody, arrived at my home. (2) A handsome, lovable golden retriever, he was everything I had hoped for when I decided to get a service dog and so much more.

(3) I have muscular dystrophy a disease that attacks your muscles and makes them very weak. (4) Because of this weakness, I am confined to a wheelchair and have difficulty using my hands and arms. (5) Before Cody came, I felt useless and unable to do the simplest things myself. (6) I needed help with even the most common tasks, from opening doors to picking up a dropped pen.

(7) All of that changed once Cody arrived. (8) Cody opens doors and drawers and helps me get my clothes out of the drier. (9) If I drop anything, he picks it up and sets it in my lap. (10) He even takes my socks off for me at night. (11) He has given me back my independence.

(12) Cody has also revived my self-confidence. (13) I used to go to great lengths to avoid going out by myself. (14) It just seems easier to stay at home and not to bother even trying. (15) Now, I go out feeling confident that I can take care of myself as long as Cody is by my side. (16) If you're in a wheelchair, people tend to look through you as if you're not even there. (17) Things are different now. (18) Whether I'm in the mall or sitting outside, people come up and talk. (19) At first they want to know about Cody, but then they want to know about me. (20) I'm meeting new people all the time, and some of them have become good friends.

(21) My constant companion is Cody, my trusted assistant, and my best friend. (22) Thanks to Cody, I think more about what I can do than about what I cannot do. (23) I am telling jokes again and making people laugh. (24) Thanks to Cody, I've begun to look forward to each and every day.

GO ON

1 What change should be made in sentence 1?

A Change *which* to **that**

B Delete the comma after *Cody*

C Change *the day* to **on the day**

D Change *arrived* to **was arriving**

2 What change, if any, should be made in sentence 3?

F Change *have* to **had**

G Change *muscles* to **mussels**

H Insert a comma after *dystrophy*

J Make no change

3 What change, if any, should be made in sentence 5?

A Change *to do* to **to have done**

B Insert a comma after *useless*

C Change *simplest* to **simpler**

D Make no change

4 What change should be made in sentence 8?

F Change *me* to **us**

G Change *drier* to **dryer**

H Change *helps* to **he helps**

J Insert a comma after *drawers*

5 What change should be made in sentence 14?

A Change *even* to **ever**

B Insert a colon after *easier*

C Change *seems* to **seemed**

D Change *bother* to **have bothered**

6 What is the correct way to rewrite sentence 21?

F My constant companion is: Cody—my trusted assistant and my best friend.

G Cody is my constant companion, my trusted assistant, and my best friend.

H My constant companion is Cody: he is my trusted assistant, and my best friend.

J Cody is my constant companion; he is my trusted assistant, he is my best friend.

Editing Practice 2

Read the following personal narrative. Then read each question and mark the correct answer.

Luz wrote this personal narrative to describe an important lesson she learned. She would like you to read her narrative and think about the corrections she should make. When you finish reading, answer the questions that follow.

My Winning Attitude

(1) I started running when I was fourteen and quickly discovered that I not only liked it but also was good at it. (2) My first 5K race was a joyous, exhilarating experience. (3) I placed third and after that got serious about training. (4) I ran three times a week, cross-trained, and did interval workouts on an indoor track. (5) I stuck to my program and didn't make excuses no matter how busy I was or bad the weather was. (6) My favorite part of running was to imagine I was an elagant cheetah, sprinting at enormous speeds across sub-Saharan plains.

(7) My hard work paid off. (8) I won my second 5K race and several other races after them, with no other runner even coming close to catching me. (9) However, after a while, I started to made excuses for not training. (10) "I'll win easily," I told myself "just like before."

(11) The best word to describe how I felt on the day of my last race is *smug*. (12) The other runners all knew who I was, and I could see them looking at me as the one they wanted to beat. (13) When the race began, I zoomed to the front; but it didn't last long. (14) Something was very wrong. (15) I didn't feel like a cheetah; I felt more like a snail lugging a huge shell. (16) I watched as other runners, one by one, passed by me. (17) I was in shock, and no amount of willing myself to run faster helped. (18) I not only lost, I got creamed.

(19) What had happened? (20) Looking back on my three years of running, I can see that winning had become more important to me than running; I had lost the exhilaration that running once gave me. (21) I was more arrogant that I thought somehow first prize belonged to me. (22) It was my attitude and not my legs that failed me. (23) Losing that race was humiliating, but it taught me an important life lesson: the joy of winning is short-lived, but the joy of doing something you love can last a lifetime.

Name _____ Date _____

1 What change, if any, should be made in sentence 1?

    A Change *started* to **had started**
    B Insert a comma after *fourteen*
    C Change *liked* to **like**
    D Make no change

2 What change should be made in sentence 5?

    F Change *to* to **near**
    G Change *bad* to **how bad**
    H Change *stuck* to **sticked**
    J Change *weather was* to **weather**

3 What change should be made in sentence 6?

    A Change *plains* to **planes**
    B Change *elagant* to **elegant**
    C Change *sub-Saharan* to **sub-saharan**
    D Replace the comma with a semicolon

4 What change should be made in sentence 8?

    F Delete *even*
    G Change *them* to **that**
    H Change *coming* to **came**
    J Change *catching* to **catch**

5 What change should be made in sentence 10?

    A Change *easily* to **easy**
    B Change *I'll win* to **I win**
    C Insert a comma after *myself*
    D Delete all the quotation marks

6 What change, if any, should be made in sentence 21?

    F Change *more* to **so**
    G Change *that* to **then**
    H Change *first prize* to **first-prize**
    J Make no change

Part II

Texas Write Source

Assessments

Pretest

Part 1: Improving Sentences and Paragraphs

Questions 1–6: Read each sentence. Choose the best way to write the underlined part of the sentence. Fill in the circle of the correct answer on your answer document.

1 <u>If a student shows special talent at playing a musical instrument, they are encouraged to join</u> the school orchestra.

  A If a student shows special talent at playing a musical instrument, he or she are encouraged to join

  B If a student shows special talent at playing a musical instrument, these are encouraged to join

  C If a student shows special talent at playing a musical instrument, he or she is encouraged to join

  D Make no change

2 <u>Despite it being made of brass, the saxophone is technically a woodwind</u> because the sound is made with a vibrating reed.

  F Although the saxophone is made of brass, it is technically a woodwind

  G When technically made of brass, the saxophone is a woodwind

  H Made of brass technically, the saxophone is a woodwind

  J Make no change

3 The local newspaper gave the orchestra high praise <u>and said they were an asset to the school and to the community</u>.

  A and said they were assets to the school and to the community

  B and said it was an asset to the school and to the community

  C and said it were an asset to the school and to the community

  D Make no change

4 The conductor remarked that although the concert was a success, it might have been even better <u>if everyone would have worked a bit harder</u>.

  F if everyone would of worked a bit harder

  G if everyone worked a bit harder

  H if everyone had worked a bit harder

  J Make no change

5 The first clarinetist had a difficult solo to play, but she practiced at home and <u>learned it real quick</u>.

   A learned it really quick

   B learned it real quickly

   C learned it really quickly

   D Make no change

6 <u>One of the trumpet players on the night before the concert, slipped on some ice, and split his lip; so he could not play.</u>

   F One of the trumpet players could not play because he slipped on some ice the night before the concert and split his lip.

   G One of the trumpet players slipped on some ice the night before the concert so he could not play and split his lip.

   H He could not play the night before the concert, so one of the trumpet players slipped on some ice and split his lip.

   J Make no change

Questions 7–8: Read each question and fill in the circle of the correct answer on your answer document.

7 Which is a complete sentence written correctly?

   A A good player who has a lot of natural talent and works hard.

   B The strings of a piano, which are struck rather than plucked or bowed.

   C A great symphony orchestra, comprising as many as one hundred players.

   D Being a good musician involves listening as well as playing.

8 Which is the best way to combine these two sentences? Some of the greatest trumpet players were jazz musicians. Louis Armstrong was the greatest jazz trumpeter of all.

   F Louis Armstrong was the greatest of all jazz trumpeters, some of whom were among the greatest jazz musicians.

   G Louis Armstrong, the greatest of all jazz trumpeters, was among some of the greatest jazz musicians.

   H Some of the greatest trumpet players were jazz musicians, among them Louis Armstrong.

   J Some of the greatest trumpet players were jazz musicians, and the greatest of them all was Louis Armstrong.

Name _____ Date _____

(1) When people say, "I was there," they are often trying to tell us they know better than we do. (2) We usually take their word for what they saw and heard, and trust their judgment. (3) They were lucky and we were not. (4) Eyewitnesses, however, can be unreliable. (5) History is sometimes a more reliable judge of great events, and its judgment can be very different from that of people who were present at the time.

(6) November 19, 1863, was the most solemn day of the Civil War. (7) More than 50,000 men had died at the Battle of Gettysburg four months before. (8) More than 23,000 Union soldiers had been buried in the new cemetery. (9) The new cemetery was built on the battle site. (10) More than 20,000 people came that day to hear Edward Everett, the most famous speaker of the age, pay tribute to those fallen soldiers. (11) The committee in charge of the ceremony had invited President Abraham Lincoln almost as an afterthought to give "a few appropriate remarks."

(12) Lincoln did not have a lot of time to prepare a long speech, but he jotted down his thoughts on the back of an envelope. (13) Some people think that the crowd did not realize the speech had even started when it was over. (14) Edward Everett's speech took two hours to deliver, and Lincoln talked for just over two minutes. (15) Was the crowd expecting more? (16) As he sat down, Lincoln said to a friend, "It is a flat failure, and the people are disappointed." (17) The *Chicago Times* described Lincoln's speech as "silly, flat, and dishwatery." (18) History judges the Gettysburg Address very differently.

9 Which sentence is not relevant to the writer's argument and should be removed?

- **A** We usually take their word for what they saw and heard, and trust their judgment.
- **B** They were lucky and we were not.
- **C** Eyewitnesses, however, can be unreliable.
- **D** History is sometimes a more reliable judge of great events, and its judgment can be very different from that of people who were present at the time.

10 Which is the best way to combine the two underlined sentences (8 and 9)?

- **F** More than 23,000 Union soldiers had been buried in the new cemetery, which was built on the battle site.
- **G** More than 23,000 Union soldiers, built on the battle site, had been buried in the new cemetery.
- **H** More than 23,000 Union soldiers had been buried in the new cemetery, it was built on the battle site.
- **J** More than 23,000 Union soldiers had been buried in the new cemetery that they had built on the battle site.

GO ON

11 Which sentence from the passage is an interrogative sentence?

    A sentence 1

    B sentence 7

    C sentence 13

    D sentence 15

12 Which would be the best word or phrase to insert into sentence 18 to link it to sentences 16 and 17?

    F As a result,

    G However,

    H Nonetheless,

    J In spite of them,

13 Which of these would be the best sentence to insert before sentence 12 to introduce the third paragraph?

    A To many of those present that day, Lincoln's remarks were too few and not exactly appropriate.

    B Lincoln's "appropriate remarks" were delivered to a crowd of people who came to hear Edward Everett.

    C Even though President Lincoln was an afterthought, he made some remarks.

    D Lincoln's remarks were few, and his appearance that day was really not appropriate.

14 Which sentence should be added after sentence 18 to conclude this piece?

    F This proves just how wrong eyewitnesses can be.

    G It is the greatest speech ever made by an American.

    H It is now regarded as one of the greatest speeches in American history.

    J Eyewitness accounts are often valuable but not always reliable.

© Houghton Mifflin Harcourt Publishing Company

Name _____ Date _____

Questions 15–20: A student wrote this passage. It may need some changes or corrections. Read the passage. Then read each question. Fill in the circle of the correct answer on your answer document.

(1) I truly believe that vegetarianism is wrong—historically, practically, and morally. (2) If our ancestors had been vegetarians, North America as we know it would not exist. (3) About 12,000 years ago, Asia and North America were connected by a wide corridor of land known as the Bering Land Bridge. (4) Tribes of hunters crossed that bridge from Asia to America, following migrating herds of mammoths and other large mammals. (5) They did not come in search of potatoes, tomatoes, or maize! (6) Like us, they were meat eaters. (7) So were the people who created those famous cave paintings in Lascaux, France, which depict armed hunters, not farmers with spades and hoes.

(8) Animals provide essential protein and vitamins that other foods do not. (9) Only meat and fish provide vitamin B12, for example. (10) To obtain the protein contained in a pound of beef, a vegetarian would have to eat at least ten pounds of beans, twenty pounds of pasta, or thirty loaves of bread. (11) I think we can all agree that this is impractical, ridiculous, and immoral.

(12) Nature has provided us with a sumptuous feast, and we would be ungrateful to pick and choose what we want and don't want. (13) Besides, if we did not keep pigs, cattle, and sheep for food, they would run wild all over the place. (14) I think this proves my point and completes my proof that vegetarianism is wrong—historically, practically, and morally.

15 What type of passage is this?

   A argumentative

   B expository

   C personal narrative

   D interpretive response to literature

16 What pattern of organization does the writer use to organize these two paragraphs?

   F problem and solution

   G cause and effect

   H thesis with supporting examples

   J chronological order

17 Which would be the best word or phrase to insert at the beginning of sentence 8 to help make the transition to the ideas in the next paragraph?

A Furthermore,

B Technically speaking,

C It is well known that

D In practical terms,

18 Which sentence is inappropriate and should be removed from this passage?

F They did not come in search of potatoes, tomatoes, or maize!

G Only meat and fish provide vitamin B12, for example.

H To obtain the protein contained in a pound of beef, a vegetarian would have to eat at least ten pounds of beans, twenty pounds of pasta, or thirty loaves of bread.

J Besides, if we did not keep pigs, cattle, and sheep for food, they would run wild all over the place.

19 Which sentence could best be inserted before sentence 8 to add to readers' understanding?

A Meat always has been and always will be part of the human diet.

B Meat is better than vegetarian food.

C A meat eater's diet has more nutritional value than a vegetarian diet.

D Pound for pound, meat beats vegetables every time.

20 If this passage continued, what information would be most logical to add in the next paragraph of the passage?

F comments explaining the drawbacks of vegetarianism

G some contrasts between the personalities of meat eaters and vegetarians

H humane ways of raising farm animals

J some personal experiences with meat eaters and vegetarians

© Houghton Mifflin Harcourt Publishing Company

GO ON

Part 2: Correcting Sentence Errors

Questions 21–26: Read each sentence. One of the underlined parts may be an error in grammar or usage. Decide which underlined part, if any, should be corrected. Fill in the circle of the correct answer on your answer document.

21 This book, *Health Tips for the Summer*,
                       A

  <u>says</u> that <u>it's important</u> to use a sunscreen
  B   **C**

in <u>a hot, sunny</u> place such as Florida.
       D

<u>Make no change.</u>
    E

22 We really enjoyed <u>the holiday</u>, and when we
                F

<u>got home</u>, I wrote a letter <u>thanking</u> Maya for
 G   **H**

inviting <u>Celia and I</u> to her family's
     J

Thanksgiving. <u>Make no change.</u>
         K

23 <u>I have never said</u> that I <u>could see</u> as well as
     A   **B**

a wildcat, but I <u>have known</u> from long
            C

experience in the mountains that my hearing

<u>is</u> much sharper than a bear's.
D

<u>Make no change.</u>
    E

24 Aunt Emily <u>used to say</u> that she
         F

<u>didn't never prefer</u> sitting out on the porch
       G

to <u>being inside</u> the house
    H

<u>watching television.</u> <u>Make no change.</u>
     J   **K**

25 The <u>sherrif</u> <u>never stood by</u> and
     A   **B**

<u>watched when</u> he saw <u>an injustice</u>, even
   C   **D**

when his own life was at risk.

<u>Make no change.</u>
    E

26 Claudia <u>promised</u> that she <u>would help me</u>
     F   **G**

install some new software <u>yesterday</u>:
                 H

<u>unfortunately</u>, she never showed up.
  J

<u>Make no change.</u>
    K

Pretest
© Houghton Mifflin Harcourt Publishing Company

GO ON ▶

Part 3: Writing   Narrative

READ

One of the best feelings we can have is the feeling we get when we do something very special for someone else. Similarly, we are often deeply affected when someone does something special for us.

THINK

Think of a time when you did something special for someone else—or when someone else did something special for you. Consider how the experience changed or affected you.

WRITE

Write a personal narrative telling what special thing you or the other person did and how the experience affected your life.

As you write your composition, remember to —

☐ write a thoughtful and engaging narrative, making use of literary techniques and devices such as dialogue and suspense

☐ develop one central conflict through its climax and resolution

☐ recount events in an order that makes sense, and make that order clear to readers

☐ make sure your composition is no longer than one page

© Houghton Mifflin Harcourt Publishing Company

Progress Test 1

Part 1: Improving Sentences and Paragraphs

Questions 1–6: Read each sentence. Choose the best way to write the underlined part of the sentence. Fill in the circle of the correct answer on your answer document.

1 In 1215, a document known as the Magna Carta was signed by King John, <u>that</u> needed to control the rebellious nobles of England.

  A which

  B whom

  C who

  D Make no change

2 The Magna Carta stated that the king <u>could</u> only rule with the consent of the people and had to obey the laws of the land.

  F may

  G shall

  H can

  J Make no change

3 King John had to choose between civil war and appeasement, and he chose <u>the best</u> of the two options.

  A the better

  B the good

  C well

  D Make no change

4 The influence of the Magna Carta can be seen very <u>clear</u> in the U.S. Constitution and the Bill of Rights.

  F clarity

  G clearly

  H clearer

  J Make no change

© Houghton Mifflin Harcourt Publishing Company

GO ON ➡

5 Although some kings and queens were unwilling to obey the law, the terms of the Magna Carta had to be renewed, revised, and enlarged many times over the centuries.

A Despite

B In fact

C Because

D Make no change

6 The Magna Carta, which controlled the powers of monarchs, are regarded by historians as one of the first stirrings of the democratic spirit.

F were

G will be

H is

J Make no change

Questions 7–8: Read each question and fill in the circle of the correct answer on your answer document.

---

7 Which is a run-on sentence that should be written as two sentences?

A King John gave the document his royal seal in a meadow at Runnymede, a village on the Thames River to the west of London.

B The Pope objected strongly to the Magna Carta because he felt that it weakened King John's power over his subjects.

C The Pope felt that the Church's power in England would be threatened if the king lost control over his troublesome subjects.

D King John had no intention of honoring the Magna Carta almost before the ink was dry he rejected it and thus brought about a bitter civil war.

8 Which is an interrogative sentence that should end with a question mark?

F Was what he did short-sighted and self-destructive

G A group of powerful barons joined together and marched into London with their combined armies on June 10, 1215

H The barons demanded that King John respect what they believed were their rights

J King John asked himself how he could keep his powers and still avoid civil war

© Houghton Mifflin Harcourt Publishing Company

> **Questions 9–14 refer to the following passage. Read the passage. Then read each question. Fill in the circle of the correct answer on your answer document.**

(1) A few days ago, I asked my friend Keiko to name her favorite book. (2) Keiko is a Japanese student from Tokyo. (3) She has come to study here in Dallas for a year. (4) Without hesitation, she replied that Jane Austen's *Pride and Prejudice* was the book she admired and loved more than any other.

(5) I was amazed. (6) How could a book written in 1813 appeal so strongly to someone of the twenty-first century? (7) How could a story about genteel ladies and wealthy gentlemen in the English countryside have such an effect on a Japanese girl from one of the busiest, most cosmopolitan cities in the world?

(8) "I guess you must like to learn about English society in the nineteenth century," I said.

(9) "That's fun," she replied, "but that's not why I like it so much."

(10) Keiko had a copy of the book in her bag. (11) She opened it and pointed to the first sentence on the first page: "It is a universal truth that a single man with a large fortune is in need of a wife."

(12) "That statement is as interesting today as it was in 1813," she said. (13) "It is certainly true in Japan, even though many in America would say it is not true here. (14) The characters in the book are people we still recognize today, and their problems and emotions are the same as ours. (15) I'm sure you could find modern versions of Elizabeth Bennet and Mr. Darcy here in Dallas. (16) A good novel is timeless, and if it is true to human nature, then it is universally true."

(17) "Is it funny, too?" I asked.

(18) "It's hilarious," she replied.

9 What kind of passage is this?

- **A** argumentative
- **B** expository
- **C** interpretive response to literature
- **D** personal narrative

10 What pattern of organization did the writer use in this passage?

- **F** comparison and contrast
- **G** chronological order
- **H** problem and solution
- **J** order of importance

GO ON

11 What is the best way to combine sentences 2 and 3?

   A Keiko is a Japanese student from Tokyo who has come to study here in Dallas for a year.

   B Keiko is a Japanese student come from Tokyo to study here in Dallas for a year.

   C Keiko is a Japanese student who has come to study here in Dallas for a year from Tokyo.

   D Keiko is a Japanese student, here in Dallas to study from Tokyo for a year.

12 In the sixth paragraph, which is the topic sentence?

   F "That statement is as interesting today as it was in 1813."

   G "It is certainly true in Japan, even though many in America would say it is not true here."

   H "The characters are people we still recognize today, and their problems and emotions are the same as ours."

   J "I'm sure you could find modern versions of Elizabeth Bennet and Mr. Darcy here in Dallas."

13 Which sentence could best be added after sentence 4 to provide useful detail?

   A She said she much preferred it to other novels.

   B She said she liked the movie version, too.

   C She told me she had actually started reading it again that day.

   D She said she particularly liked the American paperback version.

14 Which sentence could best be added at the beginning of sentence 12 to link it to the preceding paragraph?

   F Then she smiled and closed the book.

   G Keiko slammed the book shut and laughed out loud.

   H "I really love that sentence, don't you?"

   J Keiko read on silently, forgetting that I was there.

GO ON

Questions 15–20: A student wrote this passage. It may need some changes or corrections. Read the passage. Then read each question. Fill in the circle of the correct answer on your answer document.

(1) Bullying can be a real problem in school—and I should know, because I used to be a bully myself. (2) We have other problems in our school, too. (3) I used to bully kids I thought were smarter than I was. (4) I didn't use any kind of physical force. (5) I just used to point out to them forcefully that being smart wasn't the most important thing in the world, and that I could be smarter than they were if I put my mind to it. (6) I said I was just too busy doing other more interesting things and didn't care to show off my intellectual prowess. (7) In reality, I wasn't.

(8) A new kid came to our school in the eighth grade. (9) He was kind of a loner like me, and I liked him. (10) We became friends. (11) The funny thing was, this kid was smart, and for some reason he thought I was smart, too. (12) I had never given myself a chance to find out if I was smart or not I just pretended that it didn't really matter. (13) Then I began to think it was actually pretty cool to be smart. (14) That was when I started working hard, and that was when I stopped bullying other kids. (15) I guess I discovered I wasn't stupid.

15 What kind of passage is this?

A argumentative
B expository
C interpretive response to literature
D editorial

16 Which sentence is inappropriate and should be removed from this passage?

F We have other problems in our school, too.
G In reality, I wasn't.
H The funny thing was, this kid was smart, and for some reason he thought I was smart, too.
J Then I began to think it was actually pretty cool to be smart

17 Which would be the best sentence to insert at the beginning of sentence 8 to link it to sentence 7?

A Then everything changed.
B Soon after my sixteenth birthday, my school changed.
C I soon learned the error of my ways.
D I was going downhill fast.

GO ON

18 Which is a run-on sentence that should be written as two sentences?

   F Bullying can be a real problem in school—and I should know, because I used to be a bully myself.

   G I just used to point out to them forcefully that being smart wasn't the most important thing in the world, and that I could be smarter than they were if I put my mind to it.

   H I had never given myself a chance to find out if I was smart or not I just pretended that it didn't really matter.

   J That was when I started working hard, and that was when I stopped bullying other kids.

19 Which is the best way to rewrite sentences 14 and 15 to conclude the passage?

   A That was when I started working hard. I stopped bullying other kids because I guess I discovered I wasn't stupid.

   B That was when I started working hard and guessed I wasn't stupid. I discovered I stopped bullying other kids.

   C That was when I started working hard. I stopped bullying other kids and discovered I wasn't stupid.

   D That was when I started working hard and discovered I wasn't stupid. That was when I stopped bullying other kids.

20 Which detail sentence could best be inserted after sentence 8 to add to the readers' understanding?

   F His name was Jason, and we got to know each other.

   G Our school actually has five different eighth-grade homerooms.

   H He lived in Philadelphia before he and his dad moved here.

   J The school I go to has a lot of students in it.

Part 2: Correcting Sentence Errors

Questions 21–26: Read each sentence. One of the underlined parts may be an error in grammar or usage. Decide which underlined part, if any, should be corrected. Fill in the circle of the correct answer on your answer document.

21 Mr. Delany, <u>whom</u> I think <u>had been teaching</u>
         A   **B**

math for <u>thirty-five</u> years, retired in July and
       C

<u>went off to live</u> in Hawaii. <u>Make no change</u>.
 D   **E**

22 The atmosphere in the clubhouse is

   <u>generally</u> quite <u>freely</u> and relaxed, and
    F   **G**

members, <u>both young and old</u>, are
        H

encouraged to say <u>what's on their minds</u>.
            J

<u>Make no change</u>.
   K

23 When Mario and Anna <u>came out of</u> the café,
              A

they were <u>horrified to</u> <u>discover that</u>
        B   **C**

someone had stolen <u>there</u> bikes from the
           D

rack on the sidewalk. <u>Make no change</u>.
              E

24 <u>On Mondays</u>, I look after my sister <u>while</u> my
  F   **G**

mom goes to <u>yoga</u> classes, and on Fridays,
      H

I take care of a <u>neighbor's dog</u> while he
        J

goes to Swedish lessons. <u>Make no change</u>.
             K

25 Herman Melville, the great American author

who wrote '<u>Moby Dick</u>,' was so
       A

<u>little-known</u> when he died in 1891 that
 B

The New York Times referred to him as
        C

"<u>Henry Melville</u>" in an obituary.
    D

<u>Make no change</u>.
  E

26 The woodland badger is such a

<u>timid, secretive</u> animal that
    F

<u>it won't never</u> come out in the daytime when
 G

<u>there are people</u> <u>around</u>. <u>Make no change</u>.
  H   **J**   **K**

© Houghton Mifflin Harcourt Publishing Company

Questions 27–32: Read the passage. Choose the best way to write each underlined part. Fill in the circle of the correct answer on your answer document.

Dear Ms. Carroll,

I am writing to tell you how sorry I am about what happened on Friday.

I realize that pet <u>owner's</u> must take responsibility for their animals, and most
27
of the time I am very careful to make sure I know what Gus is doing. Gus

didn't know he was digging up your <u>prize geraniums?</u> He is usually very
28
<u>respectfull</u> of other people's property. He is also sympathetic to people's
29
feelings, and he would be sad if he knew he had upset you.

I think you would like Gus if you really got to know <u>him; he</u> is a fine dog with
30
an excellent temperament. He only barks when he's excited or something has

frightened him. He's very clean, and <u>he's very good with childrens, too</u>.
31
Once more, I apologize for what happened, and I promise it will never

happen again.

<u>sincerely yours,</u>
32
Anne Billson

GO ON

27 A owners
   B owners'
   C owners's
   D Make no change

28 F prize geraniums!
   G prize geraniums.
   H prize-geraniums?
   J Make no change

29 A respeckful
   B respectfully
   C respectful
   D Make no change

30 F him: he
   G him—he
   H him, he
   J Make no change

31 A he's very good with childs, too
   B hes very good with childrens, too
   C he's very good with children, too
   D Make no change

32 F sincerely Yours,
   G Sincerely yours,
   H Sincerely Yours,
   J Make no change

GO ON

Part 3: Writing   Expository

READ

Although much has been done in recent years to reduce the number of students who fail to finish high school, dropout rates are still too high in nearly every part of the United States.

THINK

Think about the circumstances that might cause a student to leave school before graduation. Consider whether these circumstances are preventable or unavoidable.

WRITE

Write an expository essay in which you clearly explain some of the causes of high dropout rates in high schools. Give examples to strengthen your essay.

As you write your composition, remember to —

☐ include a thesis statement that explains the causes of high dropout rates in high schools

☐ organize your ideas in a logical order, and connect those ideas using transitions

☐ develop your ideas fully and thoughtfully with well-chosen examples and observations

☐ make sure your composition is no longer than one page

Progress Test 2

Part 1: Improving Sentences and Paragraphs

Questions 1–6: Read each sentence. Choose the best way to write the underlined part of the sentence. Fill in the circle of the correct answer on your answer document.

1 Samuel Langhorne Clemens, <u>which</u> was born in Florida, Missouri, drew on his boyhood experiences along the Mississippi for many of his stories.

   A that was

   B whom was

   C who was

   D Make no change

2 Clemens adopted the name "Mark Twain" because <u>it's</u> the words that riverboat men used for a depth of "two fathoms" of water.

   F it was

   G it were

   H they were

   J Make no change

3 Mark Twain used his brief experience as a Confederate militiaman <u>about</u> one of his earliest short stories, *The Private History of a Campaign That Failed*.

   A in

   B around

   C into

   D Make no change

4 *The Adventures of Huckleberry Finn* <u>deal</u> seriously with issues of race, slavery, and the abuse of children.

   F dealing

   G deals

   H dealed

   J Make no change

5 Mark Twain once remarked that he never <u>let</u> schooling get in the way of his education.

A letting

B letted

C lets

D Make no change

6 Despite his success, Mark Twain was never <u>wisely</u> with money or business matters and often found himself in financial trouble.

F wiser

G wise

H wiseliest

J Make no change

Questions 7–8: Read each question and fill in the circle of the correct answer on your answer document.

7 What is the best way to combine these two sentences?

> Samuel Clemens used several pen names. Samuel Clemens sometimes wrote under the name "Sieur Louis de Conte."

A Samuel Clemens used several pen names, he sometimes wrote under the name "Sieur Louis de Conte."

B Samuel Clemens used several pen names, including the name "Sieur Louis de Conte."

C Samuel Clemens used several pen names, and Clemens sometimes wrote under the name "Sieur Louis de Conte."

D "Sieur Louis de Conte" was among the pen names Samuel Clemens used, and he used several.

8 Which is the best way to improve this sentence to make it more interesting?

> Mark Twain listened to other Americans speak.

F Mark Twain, the author, was also a person who listened to other Americans speak.

G Mark Twain often listened to other Americans, who tended to speak a lot.

H Mark Twain, who listened to other Americans speak, was an excellent speaker, listener, and writer.

J Mark Twain listened carefully to the way his fellow Americans spoke, and he used that knowledge to write great dialogue.

GO ON

Questions 9–14 refer to the following passage. Read the passage. Then read each question. Fill in the circle of the correct answer on your answer document.

(1) In 1963, William Mann, the music critic of *The Times* newspaper of London, wrote that John Lennon and Paul McCartney were "the greatest songwriters since Schubert." (2) His remarks caused an uproar on both sides of the Atlantic. (3) Lovers of classical music wrote letters to the paper demanding Mann's dismissal.

(4) Franz Schubert was born in 1797 in Vienna and died there thirty-one years later. (5) He composed nearly one thousand songs. (6) Some of the songs weren't all that terrific. (7) Schubert's range was enormous, from tender love songs to raucous party rousers, and from light comedy to the darkest tragedy. (8) He was much-loved during his lifetime and is now considered one of the greatest composers who ever lived.

(9) By comparison, John Lennon and Paul McCartney wrote over two hundred songs for the Beatles. (10) Their emotional range went from the simple exuberance of "She Loves You" to the lyrical beauty of "The Long and Winding Road," and from the gentle fun of "When I'm Sixty-Four" to the brooding menace of "A Day in the Life." (11) During the brief time the Beatles were together, they were idolized by millions of fans.

(12) Nowadays, not many people would argue with Mann's judgment. (13) In all probability, Schubert would not argue either—and for the record, Paul McCartney is a great fan of Schubert!

9 Which is the best sentence to insert before sentence 1 to make the introductory paragraph more appealing to readers?

A Were the Beatles as great as Franz Schubert?

B It is difficult to say who the best this or that was, in almost any category.

C The Beatles were so much better than Schubert!

D Comparisons are always hard to make, especially between artists of different eras.

10 Which detail sentence could best be added after sentence 11?

F In the years since "Beatlemania," Lennon and McCartney's reputations as songwriters have grown.

G We now recognize that the music of the Beatles is only a small part of our culture.

H Paul McCartney was given a knighthood by Queen Elizabeth II in 1997, making him *Sir* Paul McCartney.

J John Lennon was murdered in New York City in 1980, right in front of his apartment building.

11 Which word or phrase should be added to the beginning of sentence 5 to link it with sentence 4?

    A Nevertheless,

    B On the other hand,

    C In his short lifetime,

    D However,

12 Which is the best sentence to insert before sentence 4 to introduce the ideas in the second paragraph?

    F Vienna was the capital of Austria at the time.

    G To understand the fuss, we should first learn something about history.

    H Who was William Mann, really, and why did he say that?

    J Who was Schubert, and why did Mann's remark cause such a fuss?

13 Which sentence is inappropriate and should be removed from this passage?

    A His remarks caused an uproar on both sides of the Atlantic.

    B Franz Schubert was born in 1797 in Vienna and died there thirty-one years later.

    C Some of the songs weren't all that terrific.

    D Nowadays, not many people would argue with Mann's judgment.

14 What pattern of organization did the writer use in this passage?

    F chronological order

    G classification

    H comparison and contrast

    J order of location

© Houghton Mifflin Harcourt Publishing Company

Name _____ Date _____

Questions 15–20: A student wrote this passage. It may need some changes or corrections. Read the passage. Then read each question. Fill in the circle of the correct answer on your answer document.

(1) Oscar Wilde, the nineteenth-century writer, once said that England and the United States were "two nations, divided by a common language." (2) Wilde died in Paris in 1900 after a short, tragic life. (3) Wilde's remark is a paradox: how can two nations be divided by something they share? (4) He was wittily making the point that though English and American people both speak English, the English they speak is not quite the same. (5) Some of the variations are unimportant, but some reveal deep historical and cultural differences between the two nations.

(6) Many of us know that in Britain, people put air in their "tyres," rather than their tires. (7) They look under their cars' "bonnets" to inspect the engine, not under their hoods. (8) They store things in the "boot" and not in the trunk. (9) Wear "trousers," not pants, and an Englishman's "vest" is his undershirt.

(10) Other differences run deeper. (11) Americans often refer to their neighbors across the Atlantic as "British." (12) The people who inhabit the British Isles rarely refer to themselves in this way. (13) The people of Scotland call themselves "Scots," or "Scottish" (never "Scotch"). (14) The English, the Welsh, and the Northern Irish follow the same principle—and it is important to remember that the people of the Republic of Ireland are not British at all. (15) When the four countries are united as a nation, in the Olympics, for instance, then they call themselves British—but never "Brits."

15 What kind of passage is this?

  A argumentative

  B expository

  C personal narrative

  D interpretive response to literature

16 Which sentence is not relevant and should be removed from the passage?

  F sentence 2

  G sentence 4

  H sentence 9

  J sentence 14

GO ON

17 Which sentence could best be inserted after sentence 9?

A We fly in airplanes, while they fly in "aeroplanes."

B None of these differences, though, should cause serious misunderstandings.

C After all, the people now called Americans were British colonists at one time.

D The people in England drive on the wrong side of the road.

18 Which would be the best word or phrase to insert at the beginning of sentence 10 to link it to sentence 9?

F Nonetheless,

G On the contrary,

H However,

J To be sure,

19 Which of these is a sentence fragment that should be rewritten or combined with another sentence?

A sentence 6

B sentence 7

C sentence 8

D sentence 9

20 What concluding sentence could best be added after sentence 15?

F Of course, their preferences don't really matter.

G Do Americans call themselves "Yanks"?

H They regard the word "Brit" as rude foreign slang.

J Some words used by English speakers are simply not acceptable to them.

GO ON

Part 2: Correcting Sentence Errors

Questions 21–26: Read each sentence. One of the underlined parts may be an error in grammar or usage. Decide which underlined part, if any, should be corrected. Fill in the circle of the correct answer on your answer document.

21 "I <u>would really</u> like to <u>go riding</u> with you
      A   B

on Saturday," said Jim, "<u>But</u> my bike
                 C

<u>is being repaired,</u> and it won't be ready until
    D

Monday." <u>Make no change.</u>
         E

22 My aunt claims that her grandfather clock is

a wonderful antique, <u>but I was unable</u> to
               F

<u>get to sleep</u> until about <u>three o'clock</u>
  G   H

this morning because of <u>it's</u> ticking.
              J

<u>Make no change.</u>
    K

23 <u>From the way</u> he dresses and
    A

<u>his conservative</u> hairstyle, <u>you wouldn't</u>
    B   C

<u>never</u> guess he <u>was</u> one of the biggest rock
            D

stars in the world. <u>Make no change.</u>
            E

24 <u>Was Dad able</u> to see better, he <u>would not</u>
    F   G

<u>have to wear</u> the thick <u>tri-focal glasses</u>
                 H

<u>his optician</u> prescribed for him.
    J

<u>Make no change.</u>
    K

25 When <u>I said</u> I <u>didn't want</u> to go shopping on
        A   B

<u>Saturday,</u> I really <u>meant</u> it. <u>Make no change.</u>
    C   D   E

26 Elisa <u>didn't want to go</u> home alone after the
            F

movie because <u>they were</u> getting dark, so
            G

she <u>tagged along</u> with <u>Mary and me</u>.
      H   J

<u>Make no change.</u>
    K

GO ON

Questions 27–32: Read the passage. Choose the best way to write each underlined part. Fill in the circle of the correct answer on your answer document.

I get really tired of hearing people talk about how much better things

were in the old days. When exactly were these "old days" they're referring to?

They never quite say, <u>do they.</u> Whenever the old days were, I understand
                        27

there was no crime, no pollution, no <u>violince</u> on TV, and no loud music.
                                        28

These complainers also forget the other things they were <u>missing;</u> washing
                                                            29

machines, computers, cheap air travel, heart transplants, and so on. Also,

American society is much more open and tolerant these <u>days: at least</u>
                                                        30

compared to the way it used to be.

On Thursday evenings, I do some gardening for our neighbor, Mrs.

Percival, who must be about ninety. She likes to talk about the old days. Last

week, she <u>complemented</u> me on how nice the lawn looked. I then pointed out
            31

to her that no one had riding mowers in the old days. <u>Laughing and said</u>
                                                        32

<u>they're too noisy anyway.</u>

27 A do they?
   B do they!
   C does they.
   D Make no change

28 F violence
   G vilince
   H vilence
   J Make no change

29 A missing,
   B missing:
   C missing.
   D Make no change

30 F days. At least
   G days; at least
   H days—at least
   J Make no change

31 A commented
   B complimented
   C completed
   D Make no change

32 F Laughing, she said they're too noisy anyway.
   G Laughing, and she said they're too noisy anyway.
   H She laughing and saying they're too noisy anyway.
   J Make no change

© Houghton Mifflin Harcourt Publishing Company

Part 3: Writing   Narrative

READ

Solitude—being alone—is an experience we all have at some point. Solitude may be welcome at times; we may need or enjoy the peace and quiet that comes with being alone. At other times, being alone can lead to feelings of loneliness or emptiness.

THINK

Think about a time when you experienced solitude. What were the specific circumstances? Recall whether the experience was welcome or unwelcome, pleasant or unpleasant.

WRITE

Write a personal narrative describing in detail your experience with solitude.

As you write your composition, remember to —

☐ write a thoughtful and engaging narrative, making use of literary techniques and devices such as dialogue and suspense

☐ develop one central conflict through its climax and resolution

☐ recount events in an order that makes sense, and make that order clear to readers

☐ make sure your composition is no longer than one page

STOP

Post-test

Part 1: Improving Sentences and Paragraphs

Questions 1–6: Read each sentence. Choose the best way to write the underlined part of the sentence. Fill in the circle of the correct answer on your answer document.

1 The wolverine is not related to the wolf, although the <u>two animals has</u> some similarities.

    A two animal has
    B two animals having
    C two animals have
    D Make no change

2 Last year, a six-man team of researchers spent months exploring the sub-Arctic tundra, <u>but none of the team were</u> lucky enough to see a wolverine.

    F then none of the team were
    G but none of the team was
    H even though none of the team are
    J Make no change

3 The researchers found that in the wild, wolverines <u>never eat more than they needed</u> to stay alive.

    A never ate more than they need
    B never eating more than they needed
    C never eat more than they need
    D Make no change

4 Wolverines can stay completely still for many hours at a time, but when they move, they are <u>exceptional quick</u>.

    F exceptionally quick
    G exceptional quickly
    H exceptionally quickly
    J Make no change

© Houghton Mifflin Harcourt Publishing Company

5 Wolverines are the only creatures of the Arctic and sub-Arctic that dare to attack <u>bear, who are otherwise unchallenged</u> in those desolate regions.

A the bear, who is otherwise unchallenged

B bears, which are otherwise unchallenged

C bear, which is otherwise unchallenged

D Make no change

6 <u>According to one story, a wolverine once broke into a trapper's hut, took his snowshoes, and hung them high in a tree!</u>

F A wolverine once broke into a hut, took a trapper's snowshoes according to one story, and hung them high in a tree!

G According to one story, a wolverine once broke into a trapper's hut, took his snowshoes high in a tree, and hung them!

H A wolverine once broke into a trapper's hut according to one story, took his snowshoes, and hung him high in a tree!

J Make no change

Questions 7–8: Read each question and fill in the circle of the correct answer on your answer document.

7 Which is a complete sentence written correctly?

A The native people of the region using the wolverine's thick fur to line their parkas.

B Despite its big furry paws, the wolverine has to sprint to stay on top of the snow, otherwise sinking down into it.

C The bear at the top of the food chain, but the wolverine is smart and fearless.

D Like the weasel, to which it is closely related, the wolverine is very shy.

8 Which is the best way to combine these two sentences?

> The wolverine does not chase its prey, because its eyesight is poor. The wolverine lies in hiding to ambush its prey.

F Because its eyesight is poor, the wolverine lies in hiding to ambush its prey and then chase it.

G Because its eyesight is poor, the wolverine lies in hiding to ambush its prey instead of chasing it.

H Rather than chase it, because its eyesight is poor, the wolverine lies in hiding to ambush its prey.

J The wolverine's eyesight is so poor that, rather than chasing or hiding its prey, it lies to ambush it.

© Houghton Mifflin Harcourt Publishing Company

Name _____ Date _____

(1) Francisco de Goya was a famous Spanish painter. (2) In one of his most famous works, a man is asleep at his desk. (3) He is slumped forward, his head in his hands. (4) Around him there is darkness. (5) In that darkness, creatures of the night are closing in on the man, as you might imagine in a nightmare. (6) A pen and paper lie abandoned in front of him, and some words appear on the side of his desk. (7) The words say, "The sleep of reason produces monsters." (8) This picture was created in 1797 at the end of a period known as the "Age of Reason."

(9) Goya was born in 1746 and died in 1828. (10) His early works show aristocratic ladies and gentlemen in civilized landscapes and sumptuous drawing rooms. (11) His later works show an altogether different sensibility. (12) The corrupt Spanish monarchy was overthrown by the French and then forcibly restored, <u>or</u> the leaders of the Spanish Inquisition tortured and executed thousands of Spaniards. (13) Meanwhile, famine and crime ravaged the land.

(14) Goya recorded the times he lived in. (15) He was sometimes harsh and often satirical, but he was always true to his vision. (16) He was also profoundly deaf in later years. (17) He recorded scenes of violence and terror, but there is a haunting beauty to his work. (18) Was he, as critics believe, the "Father of Modern Art"? (19) Many twentieth-century artists recognized Goya as a fellow spirit in a world in which, once again, the sleep of reason produced monsters.

9 Which sentence is not relevant to the writer's argument and should be removed?

A He is slumped forward, his head in his hands.

B His early works show aristocratic ladies and gentlemen in civilized landscapes and sumptuous drawing rooms.

C He was also profoundly deaf in later years.

D Many twentieth-century artists recognized Goya as a fellow spirit in a world in which, once again, the sleep of reason produced monsters.

10 Which is the best conjunction to use in place of the underlined <u>or</u> in sentence 12?

F and

G so

H but

J thus

11 Which sentence from the passage is an interrogative sentence?

- **A** sentence 5
- **B** sentence 8
- **C** sentence 10
- **D** sentence 18

12 Which detail sentence could best be added between sentences 11 and 12?

- **F** He was the greatest painter of his time.
- **G** One of his favorite models was the duchess of Alba.
- **H** Goya lived through a tragic period of Spanish history.
- **J** Many of his best works now hang in a museum in Madrid.

13 Which of these would be the best sentence to insert before sentence 9 to introduce the second paragraph?

- **A** The artist known as Goya grew up in Spain.
- **B** Who was Goya, and what made him produce such terrifying pictures?
- **C** Artists do not always have an easy life.
- **D** Some people think the man sleeping at his desk was actually Goya, but that is not likely.

14 What pattern of organization did the writer use to organize each paragraph in this passage?

- **F** classification
- **G** chronological order
- **H** order of location
- **J** main idea and details

© Houghton Mifflin Harcourt Publishing Company

GO ON

Name _____ Date _____

(1) "Are pets good for you?" (2) That question was asked in a magazine article I read recently. (3) It appears that the answer—according to the writer, at least—is yes! (4) Apparently, people who have a dog or a cat around the house are fitter and healthier than people who live alone.

(5) Dogs need exercise, and when a dog goes for a walk, so does its owner. (6) It is not so easy to see why pets who do not need exercise—cats, hamsters, and geckos, for example—should have any beneficial effect on their owners' health. (7) According to the writer of the article, they do. (8) She interviewed many psychiatrists and hospital doctors who encourage their patients to meet with animals, even when they are not well enough to keep one of their own.

(9) Human beings are social animals. (10) Generally speaking, they like company. (11) It must be said, some people are not easy to live with. (12) Researchers have found that solitude can cause stress. (13) Happy people are on the whole healthier than unhappy people. (14) Stress is responsible for many of the illnesses that people suffer nowadays. (15) According to the magazine article, the company of pets relieves stress and helps their owners to live healthier, happier lives.

15 What kind of passage is this?

A argumentative
B expository
C interpretive response to literature
D personal narrative

16 Which sentence is not relevant and should be removed from the passage?

F sentence 6
G sentence 8
H sentence 11
J sentence 13

17 Which sentence could best be inserted before sentence 5 to introduce the second paragraph?

A It is easy to see how a dog might keep a person fit.

B People keep all kinds of pets for all kinds of reasons.

C Dogs make very popular pets for people of all ages.

D A dog is often better company than a fitness instructor.

18 Which would be the best word or phrase to insert at the beginning of sentence 7 to link it to sentence 6?

F In spite of this,

G As a consequence,

H Not withstanding,

J Nevertheless,

19 Which two sentences should be switched to organize the third paragraph better?

A sentence 9 and sentence 10

B sentence 10 and sentence 11

C sentence 11 and sentence 12

D sentence 13 and sentence 14

20 Which concluding sentence could best be added after sentence 15?

F Many pet owners would probably agree with that sentiment.

G I have a gerbil myself, and my health is excellent.

H If you want a healthy, stress-free life, get yourself a pet!

J The article did not mention snakes and scorpions, which some people seem to enjoy as other people enjoy more conventional animal companions.

© Houghton Mifflin Harcourt Publishing Company

GO ON

Part 2: Correcting Sentence Errors

Questions 21–26: Read each sentence. One of the underlined parts may be an error in grammar or usage. Decide which underlined part, if any, should be corrected. Fill in the circle of the correct answer on your answer document.

21 My dad <u>really makes</u> great Sunday
A

<u>breakfasts: the</u> blueberry pancakes he
B

<u>makes—using</u> fresh blueberries rather than
C

frozen <u>ones—are</u> truly delicious.
D

<u>Make no change</u>.
E

22 I <u>have</u> a long list of jobs <u>I must do</u> on
F   **G**

Saturday <u>morning: clean</u> the car, go
H

shopping, pick up the dry <u>cleaning e.t.c.</u>
J

<u>Make no change</u>.
K

23 Mr. Hammond, the <u>principle</u>, called the
A

whole school together this morning <u>to say</u>
B

he was very displeased with <u>the behavior</u> of
C

some students during last

<u>Wednesday's baseball game</u>.
D

<u>Make no change</u>.
E

24 The <u>soft rubber soles</u> of the private
F

<u>detective's suede</u> loafers made no sound
G

<u>as he climbed</u> up the dark stairs to the
H

landing and crept silently past <u>one door</u> . . .
J

then another . . . and another . . . until at last

he came to the old library. <u>Make no change</u>.
K

25 Captain Brassbound lived in

<u>Bangkok Manila, and Tripoli</u> before
A   **B**

<u>settling down</u> in a small house in the
C

<u>suburbs of Houston</u>. <u>Make no change</u>.
D   **E**

26 <u>Mother and I</u> sometimes give <u>one another</u> a
F   **G**

hard time, but more often we give

<u>each other</u> words of love and
H

<u>encouragement</u>. <u>Make no change</u>.
J   **K**

GO ON

Name _____ Date _____

I really love high adventure movies, especially pirate movies. My

favorite pirate movie of all is "Pirates of the Caribbean: At World's End." It is

27

the third in this series of pirate movies, and I think it is the best yet. This

particular movie has everything you could wish for in a pirate movie—

adventure, romance, comedy, incredible special effects, and high

suspense! The locations are beautiful and exotic, the photography is

brilliant, and the acting is superb. The plot is unbelieveable; but what do

28

you expect from a pirate story? I loved every minute!

The cast has done a truly first-class job. My little sister

said, 'Johnny Depp is awesome!' I couldn't hardly have said it better myself.

29   **30**

Depp is an actor who has everything. He is handsome, talented, and

awful funny. His swashbuckling Jack Sparrow is an absolute delight. The

31

Australian actor Geoffrey Rush is suitably wicked as the villain, and Keira

Knightley and Orlando Bloom are charming and funny as the young lovers.

The first movie did very well at the box office, and the two sequels did

32

even better. The next movie in the series will undoubtedly surpass these

three.

27 A *Pirates of the Caribbean: At World's End.*

   B 'Pirates of the Caribbean: At World's End.'

   C *"Pirates of the Caribbean: At World's End."*

   D Make no change

28 F unbelievible

   G unbelievable

   H unbeleivable

   J Make no change

29 A said "Johnny Depp is awesome!"

   B said, Johnny Depp is awesome!

   C said, "Johnny Depp is awesome!"

   D Make no change

30 F could hardly have

   G couldn't hardly not have

   H could hardly not have

   J Make no change

31 A awful funnily

   B awfully funny

   C awful fun

   D Make no change

32 F very good

   G very goodly

   H real well

   J Make no change

Part 3: Writing

Expository

READ

You have probably heard someone described as being "very successful." What does being successful mean? Can success mean different things to different people, or do all of us share a similar idea of success?

THINK

Think about the meaning of the word *successful*. Consider the idea of success from different perspectives, and think about whether—and how—the meaning of the word might change.

WRITE

Write an expository essay defining what it means to be successful. Include at least two examples.

As you write your composition, remember to —

☐ include a thesis statement that defines what it means to be successful

☐ organize your ideas in a logical order, and connect those ideas using transitions

☐ develop your ideas fully and thoughtfully with well-chosen examples and observations

☐ make sure your composition is no longer than one page

© Houghton Mifflin Harcourt Publishing Company

STOP